HILL HOUSE LIVING

The art of creating a joyful life

Dedicated to:

My beautiful mother, Lydia Theodora Whiteman
2 March 1940–14 February 2020

Special mentions

My fabulous daddy – Joslyn Raphael Whiteman

My husband, who believes in me always

My children, who make me laugh daily

Coco – the star who encouraged me to show my face

HILL HOUSE LIVING

The art of creating a joyful life

@HillHouseVintage

EBURY
PRESS

Introduction: From Catwalk to
Dog Walks and Couture to Manure   6

PART 1: HILL HOUSE LIVING   16

Chapter 1: Living a Joyful Life   18

The Power of Creative
Visualisation, or Mood-boarding   22

Your Personal Style   31

The Joy of Growing and Creating   41

Chapter 2: Country House Style   46

The Old Guard – the Country House
Style of Nancy Lancaster   54

Country House Style Today   56

Race and Country House Style   58

The Relevance of Cottagecore   62

Chapter 3: The Art of Vintage Hunting   74

Becoming Hill House Vintage   78

Can Vintage Be Mixed With Modern?   90

The Hill House Guide to Vintage   92

PART 2: THE BEAUTY OF LIVING WITH THE SEASONS   112

The Seasons at Hill House   118

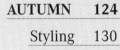

AUTUMN   124
Styling   130
Cooking   140
Making   150

WINTER   160
Styling   164
Cooking   174
Making   184

SPRING   192
Styling   196
Cooking   204
Making   212

SUMMER   216
Styling   220
Cooking   226
Making   236

Afterword   242

Notes   246

Further reading   247

Thank you   250

Index   252

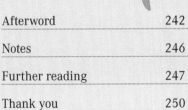

I'm just pondering how a high-heel-loving, disco-dancing, *Vogue*-buying Londoner like myself ended up becoming obsessed with old buildings, period architecture, vintage treasures and all things floral and antique. Was I always programmed to morph into a tweed-wearing character from an Enid Blyton novel, or did I fall and hit my head somewhere along the way, and awake to find that my penchant for designer shoes had been replaced by an appetite for multi-layered Victoria sponge cake overnight? Whatever the reason, give me a period property with a perfectly planted garden to drool over and a slow-paced life in the English countryside over the hustle and bustle of city living any day. From couture to manure – I've gone from catwalk to dog walk in the most literal sense ... London gave me a high-octane start, but Norfolk ended up stealing my heart! Who'd have thought that slow and steady would win the day after all!

FROM CATWALK TO DOG WALKS AND COUTURE TO MANURE

This blog post that I wrote several years ago is what initially got me thinking about writing a book. Like so many before me, I had chosen to change my life and follow my intuition. This led me to a world of self-discovery and joy. A little over a decade ago, I decided with my husband to transport our family from the busy streets of south London to a small village in Norfolk where we didn't know a soul. One day, I was stuck in traffic on the South Circular attempting to get my three children to their multicultural, thousand-pupil-strong prep school. The next, we were standing in the middle of a village playground belonging to a school that numbered only 90 students, with me and the children as the only residents of colour for miles around.

Thankfully, my leap of faith has an extremely happy and positive ending. But I've often wondered, what is it about the countryside that lures so many dedicated metropolitan types like my former self to experience a slower-paced way of living, and do you really need to move away to achieve it?

During my 20 years of working in the fashion industry in London, I produced some of the glossiest and most glamorous fashion shoots and magazine covers for one of the world's leading fashion magazines. Time and time again, despite our collective penchant for all things modern, on trend and (seemingly) sophisticated, there would be at least one fashion spread per season that would hark back to an immaculately bucolic version of the countryside. Whether it was a playful take on allotment living, 1940s Land Girl chic, Aga-baking squire or chicken-breeding debutante, the dream-filled image of the merry homesteader was ever-present. However, for me, the allure started way before then. To fully understand how and why I morphed, it's important to go back to the beginning. So here is my story ...

As the daughter of West Indian immigrants who settled in south London during the early 1960s, my love of all things country had – on first inspection – no obvious origin. But upon reflection, one clue is my mother's 'addiction' to *Country Life* magazine, which I subsequently adopted when, from an early age, I started to flick through her discarded copies.

Like me, my mother was an avid Jane Austen fan, and she had dreamed of living in a house in the English countryside. However, upon their arrival from the Caribbean, my parents' reality was a series of bedsits and lettings, followed by a slow but steady move up the property ladder, culminating in a far more modest than Pemberley-esque Edwardian house in a south London suburb. For my mother, it was the house where her dreams of acquiring her own version of an English home had finally been fulfilled, and by realising those dreams my mother provided the basis for my own romantic leanings towards English country houses and interiors that were more traditionally flavoured than the modern preferences of my contemporaries.

Despite not having come from a background where family heirlooms were passed down, I did inherit a make-do mentality. So it is perhaps unsurprising that my current decorating tastes have developed into a deep love of vintage and thrift, as well as artisan and antique. Gathered and collected (but always loved) has pretty much summed up my interior style for my entire life, and it is a mantra that I've since applied to Hill House. Regardless of age, I have always been drawn to pieces that inspire a sense of history – whether that's in the authenticity of their heritage or simply in the classic shape of their design. It's not that I do not like or own things that are new, but rather that even the new things must feel as though they could have been settled into their current position for years. These are the details that make me happy – and as my mother taught me, a happy home is everything.

Such rose-tinted dreams are all well and good when romanticising life from afar in London, but there's a distinct sense of finality on the day you pull your city front door closed for the last time, and embark on what many saw as

is everything!

sticking a pin into a map of the English countryside and hoping for the best.

Despite not having come from a background where family heirlooms were passed down, I did inherit a make-do mentality ...

But change was actually the result of much introspection and the realisation that I possessed a total inability to separate work from home life. My husband and I made the decision to move to where our theoretical 'pin' landed in a bid for our own children to live out the quiet country life that I had secretly desired since childhood. When people exclaimed at the 'bravery' of departing from the city in which I had been born and raised, I would chuckle. After all, my parents' journey had been a real leap of faith; making a move a hundred miles up the road to Norfolk – the county I now live in – hardly seemed a feat of great endurance. Ironically, even though those miles may be short in comparison to a journey across an ocean, for a fashion-loving girl used to the busyness of metropolitan living, the move to the wide-open spaces of Norfolk was culturally akin to moving from Earth to Mars.

And despite the pleasing architecture of Hill House and the grand interior and garden-landscaping ideas that lived within the vision board of my mind, the reality of having no excess budget after the purchase of the house soon hit. It became apparent that I needed to come up with some practical solutions and creative ideas to fill the empty rooms in the house and turn these spaces into something welcoming. As the children settled into school and my husband adjusted to his new commute, I was left to begin the challenge of creating the comfortable and happy family home that I knew it could be – on a threadbare budget.

Thankfully, the gathered, collected and timeworn 'underdogs' of the interiors world are the things that epitomise my interior style. Local auction houses where wooden dining chairs could be found for a fiver apiece quickly became my friend; eBay, car boot sales, old curiosity shops, vintage emporiums and antiques markets soon became my natural hunting grounds; repainting, restoring and re-covering furniture that had already lived a life became my absolute passion.

However, while my core aesthetic may be based on vintage, for me it really is all about the mix. The beauty and the eclecticism of curating your own personal style – whether that be from preloved or brand-new items – fills me with joy, and can be adapted to suit whatever budget you have. This is what I hope to show you in this book. The bonus of this style is that it's sustainable, easy to achieve, suits every lifestyle and doesn't break the bank.

Over the past decade, I have learned as many life lessons as I have decorating lessons, and in exploring both, this book will be a reflection on the beauty that can be found in everyday life. From making and cooking to styling, growing, upcycling and repurposing, the idea that our homes can become our own self-contained mini oases of calm and wellbeing resonates more than ever; I have therefore included all of these elements. It doesn't take a castle or a country estate to find happiness in your own home – most of the lessons that I've learned over the years can be applied to the smallest of spaces as much as the larger ones. Whether it's re-covering a vintage chair using remnants of old material, growing herbs and flowers in a window box, or creating a series of beautifully styled vignettes of gathered and vintage objects to add personality and individuality to your decor, the theories behind creating a curated home and garden that you love will work well whatever your circumstances.

At Hill House, I started with an empty house, a large expanse of garden and the determination to make a comfortable home. Searching for a plan, I turned to nature and was guided by the seasons. I started as an enthusiastic novice at everything, but as each season came around it unearthed the joy of following my instinct and using my imagination in my quest to carve out a new version of a happy home. Changing your life and leaping into the unknown is an optimistic pursuit, but so is staying put and making the most of what you already have.

Committing to the life that you visualise can be a grounding adventure that can reap many unexpected rewards. The good news is that you can find beauty whatever your decision – you just need a little self-belief and patience.

As a self-confessed 'slow decorator', creating my ideal spaces took time and thoughtfulness, and it is still an ongoing labour of love, passion and self-exploration. In fact, many of my spaces, such as my gallery walls, are ever-evolving works of art in themselves, a continually metamorphosing story of history and time. This is what home means to me: a map of your life, loves and hopes over the years. My aim is to share with you just how to achieve your own personal version of that map through the projects and stories that have made up a year at Hill House.

> **As a self-confessed 'slow decorator', creating my ideal spaces took time and thoughtfulness, and it is still an ongoing labour of love, passion and self-exploration.**

Above all, I believe that our spaces must always bring us joy. I hope that sharing the things that I've learned, the stories that have helped me along the way, and how the seasons have had an impact on my journey to joy will bring you pleasure, too.

Love,

PART 1

HILL HOUSE LIVING

The intention behind Hill House Living is to give you a few examples of how I have chosen to fill my life with as much beauty and positivity as I am able to, with a view to offering you some thought-provoking ideas and simple changes that may help you consider the way in which you choose to live yours. This section of the book explores my approach to wellbeing, the origins of the country house style and my tips on how to get the most out of vintage and antiques hunting.

CHAPTER 1

Living a Joyful Life

*It sounds so simple when written down on a page -
surely it's everyone's aim to live a life filled with joy?
Online, even if in not as many words, many people are asking:
what is the secret to happiness and contentment?
How can we live an authentic and joyful life
when there are so many outside influences and
obstacles seemingly working against us?*

I don't profess to have all of the answers, nor can I claim to possess the ability to be joyful at all times of the day and night, despite the happiness that I intentionally (and genuinely) portray in many of my images. But what I've discovered is that finding the ability to experience joy takes a bit of work and usually a lot of effort. It involves dedicating time to examining what it is that affects us, and the acknowledgement that this pursuit – self-care – is time well spent.

For generations, we have understood that taking care of our physical health is a good starting point on the route to longevity and wellbeing. What has been overlooked is that considering happiness and contentment in our notion of 'fitness' can go a long way in improving our health. Commuting, work stress, financial worries and family and health concerns (to name just a few) can take up so much of our headspace and affect our wellbeing. When this happens it can be difficult to find the time or resources to concentrate solely on ourselves. Personally, these things played a huge part in sucking the joy out of my life before I was able to take matters into my own hands and change my circumstances. I just wish I hadn't reached the burnout stage before I realised this.

While I am no expert on happiness and wellbeing, there are a few things that I have learned to do and focus on that have helped with my own feelings. For instance, an important thing that became very apparent to me after moving from London to the Norfolk countryside is that prior to the move I hadn't spent enough time concentrating on the way that my senses affect my mood and outlook on life. In London I was caught up in the hectic, trend-driven nature of my working life. At the time, people were being pushed to achieve as much as possible: to buy that house, have that family, maintain that career, buy that thing – and do all of these things quickly and simultaneously. There was hardly room to breathe before the next life goal 'needed' to be ticked off the list. I was fortunate enough to have a family and a nice house in south London, but I hardly saw my husband and children as I was always dashing out to the job I loved but that consumed my time in order to sustain my lifestyle, one that I had conditioned myself into believing was my only choice. A fast-paced life doesn't equip us with the necessary time or space to contemplate the things that really suit us most or enhance our life best. I had a landscaped garden that I did not sit in. I decorated a house that I spent little time in. I ate food that I did not make, and yet I still wondered why a sense of peace and contentment evaded me ...

Following our move, I came to realise that slowing down to take notice of the objects I surround myself with, the things I smell, the colours I wear and the food I eat can have a tremendous mood-enhancing effect on my daily life. Taking time to visualise the elements of your life that make you happy is an important part of taking care of and learning about yourself.

That said, it doesn't take moving out of a city to realise and implement these changes. In fact, these are all life lessons that I wish I had taken on board when I still lived in London. Learning to adapt and change should be part of everyone's 'wellbeing story'.

There are so many things in this world that we cannot control, but altering the look and feel of our immediate environment to create something cosy, stylish and luminous is something that many of us can attempt to do to regain some control and, in turn, wellbeing. Whether it's the way your home looks, the way *you* look, or how both of these things make you feel, the next few pages are all about finding out how to express yourself in ways that will encourage you to feel inspired, positive and comfortable. I've included a few tips and simple techniques that have worked for me, including visualisation, planning with intent and checklists, all of which will hopefully provide food for thought and inspire you to make changes for the better. I want to share the principles I have applied to Hill House, which over recent years have improved my day-to-day life. I hope they will do the same for you, wherever you may be.

THE POWER OF CREATIVE VISUALISATION, OR MOOD-BOARDING

When I was growing up, my father would often talk about the need to have an image of what you want your life to be like in order to get to that point. After all, he would emphasise, we wouldn't start a journey without a map or a destination point, so why should our 'journey through life' be any different? What I didn't realise at the time is that my father was simply describing a classic method of visualisation in order to focus and concentrate on an end goal. Whether you believe in creative visualisation or not, one thing that is certainly true is that mapping out your aims for a particular part of your life by using a mood board is an extremely helpful tool for streamlining everything, from decorating ideas to life goals.

This isn't just mine or my father's opinion! The idea of creative visualisation itself is nothing new and has long been practised in both Eastern and Western religions. For example, some Hindus use visualisation to achieve unity with the divine, and devotees of Shiva visualise his divine consort, Shakti, as 'a spiral of positivity within the body'. The notion of using your imagination to help shape positive attitudes towards life with the aim of guiding your everyday experience, creating a positive shift towards goals and ultimate happiness, is a technique that has been well researched and documented. Psychologists, philosophers and lifestyle gurus alike have also spoken extensively about the benefits of creative visualisation. For instance, psychiatrist Abigail Brenner, writing in *Psychology Today*, explains that: 'We all operate from our own individual point of view or perspective: a reality with which our mind feels comfortable. By realising that we can consciously and actively alter our point of view through visualising a desired outcome, we have an opportunity to shift perception in reality.' Athletes have long been encouraged to use visualisation as a means to imagine the desired outcome before it materialises. By becoming more familiar with your goals you begin to limit the fear of failure and the anxiety around it. In recent years writers like Shakti Gawain, who wrote a book called *Creative Visualization*, and Rhonda Byrne, who wrote *The Secret*, have developed a worldwide following of millions and been endorsed by people such as Oprah Winfrey. This all points to the idea that visualisation is an important aspect for setting any goal, since much of the unconscious brain is oriented around a visual construction of reality. In short, if you want to do better at something, visualising your performance improves your chances.

However, when it comes to creating a mood in a room that reflects the time of the year, it's all about the styling, and as far as I'm concerned, every season can benefit from a refresh.

Following my father's lead – as well as that of Oprah Winfrey, the queen of positive thinking herself – I've found my own ways to creatively visualise the environment and life that I feel will bring me happiness. I've adopted certain techniques because, despite organising other people for a living during my fashion days, when it comes to myself I haven't always been the most organised. For this reason I create vision boards or mood boards throughout the year in order to harness my decorating and styling ideas. It's my way of staying focused and it helps to move my thoughts on from simply being fanciful musings to becoming real-life projects, and all of that gives me a sense of satisfaction, which in turn makes me happy.

My mood boards don't always have to relate to large or dramatic projects. I'm often left in awe at the speed and skill that some of my fellow professional interiors bloggers display through changing up their homes so frequently – and nailing it perfectly every time. My style is rather more permanent and

– reassuringly for me – steady. I'm actually what I call a 'slow decorator', which means that it takes me quite a while to change things, but when I do, I am sure and committed, and rarely change my mind again for quite a while.

However, when it comes to creating a mood in a room that reflects the time of the year, it's all about the styling, and as far as I'm concerned, every season can benefit from a refresh. We are spending more time than ever in our homes these days, and no space is more in need of love than our home offices. So how about creating an inspiring home office board, perhaps based on a particular season or colourway? The point of a mood board is to add things that make *you* feel positive – not what you think ought to be on there. The process is all about examining your senses and preferences.

Of course, mood-board imagery doesn't have to be about decorating and styling. I created a mood board several years ago that depicted myriad versions of pretty raised-bed gardens. It was a project that I knew would take time to achieve – gardening is a long-haul pastime, after all – but it was a pleasure to think about it over an extended period. Whenever I came across an inspiring image or idea – whether it was a picture of somebody else's garden, or a plant or product that I could imagine being included in my own plot, I would cut out the picture and paste it into a scrapbook. The raised-bed garden in question is still in its infancy (I am not only a slow decorator, but a slow gardener, too); however, the joy I have felt in watching my vision gradually take shape has been immeasurable.

Now, it's all well and good me talking about how I create my mood boards, but talking without action is like planting a seed without watering it. Let me run you through a few examples of how you can go from imagining that room (balcony, or garden) of dreams, to manifesting it and watching the shoots of your intentions appear.

CREATE A MOOD BOARD

What is the best way to communicate your idea or vision?
I have suggested a few options below as well as a checklist of must-haves!

STEP 1: CHOOSE YOUR FORMAT

SCRAPBOOKING

This is, of course, the most straightforward way of creating your vision. Label your page and board with the project that you have in mind, start cutting out relevant images from old magazines or newspapers and get sticking with glue. The process doesn't need to be completed in one go. Take your time. Wait until you see pictures or clippings that you are genuinely drawn to. A mood board can be a series of images collected over several years or more. It can evolve, mature and change. Just go with it. The advantage here is that you can gather a collection of scrapbooks on your shelf that you can refer back to.

PINTEREST

The online sharing app and website is perfect for creating mood-board pages on your phone or computer. Its beauty is that it doesn't take up any extra space and you can source your inspiration material from all over the internet as well as from 'real life'. For example, you might visit a hotel somewhere and see a beautiful and historic wallpaper design within a colour palette that – prior to that moment – you would never have considered for your own home. You simply take a photo, open the app and pin this to your board. Everything can be saved, from images to blog and Instagram posts, newspaper articles and YouTube videos; they can then be themed and organised however you choose.

ONLINE MOOD-BOARD MAKERS

There are a multitude of online websites that allow you to create your scrapbook pages so that they look just like a real-life scrapbook but are saved on your computer. Websites such as Canva, BeFunky and Mural provide templates that are ready for you to drop your saved pictures and images into.

JOURNALLING

Mood boards don't have to be visual. You can visualise your intentions and hopes by focusing on phrases, quotes and slogans. Even a single written sentence can help concentrate your mind on a project, dream or ambition. Many people use journals such as 'one line a day', or *Wreck This Journal*.

STEP 2: CARVE OUT A QUIET SPACE

Not all of us have the luxury of a dedicated room of our own. Whether we live with our families, partners or in a shared home, it's a luxury to have our own personal space beyond the rooms that we sleep in. However, as part of our self-care it's important to try to carve out a little patch somewhere that we can associate with peace, meditation perhaps, and generally just slowing down.

If you're lucky enough to have an outdoor spot, and in particular to have access to it during clement weather, then the traditional reading nook and quiet zone can be moved outdoors when indoor space is at a premium. This could be a carefully organised cushion-filled area on your terrace, a calmingly organised set-up with yoga mat and candles on your balcony, or the luxury of a hammock placed between two trees if you want to go all out. Whatever and wherever this place is, learn the importance of dedicating time to being quiet and mindful throughout the year. Not all 'feel-good' moments have to be about socialising or high-octane activity – particularly now that we know what it's like to have those freedoms occasionally curbed for reasons beyond our own control. Finding a happy moment to slow down, relax, unwind and make sense of a complicated world while making that territory uniquely 'yours' is an important part of your year-round wellbeing.

Of course, it's important to acknowledge that many people in a shared or small home simply do not have extra space to do this. If you cannot change how much room you have, the ideas opposite might still help you to adjust the overall atmosphere of your surroundings. (If this is your situation, perhaps you can negotiate a dedicated weekly 1-2 hours when you can access a communal area for calming purposes.)

Identifying how you wish to utilise your space will be the first point of action, and with a checklist, you can narrow down what your 'quiet nook' must achieve for you.

QUIET NOOK CHECKLIST

* How much space do I really need/can I get?

* Do I need to be able to spread out physically, or is it just a case of a nice spot to sit and read or listen to music?

* Do I need to watch any online tutorials for my mindful moments?

* Is there an app, such as Headspace or Calm, that can help me along with my quiet moments?

* Do I need access to electricity or a screen or monitor?

* Do I want to learn something new?

* Do I wish to acquire a new skill (or continue with an old one), such as knitting or painting or learning the basics of a new language?

* What do I want my space to look like?

* Does it help if I am surrounded by visual imagery to concentrate on, or will I be closing my eyes and simply enjoying being in my zone?

* What do I want my space to smell like? Do I need candles, sprays and diffusers?

* What do I want my area to feel like? Do I need cushions, blankets, a screen?

* Can it be a portable place? Can I keep everything that I need in a bag or box and use it wherever I wish, or do I need my space to be permanently fixed to a certain area or room?

* Do I need shelving for books, magazines or other resources and equipment?

YOUR PERSONAL STYLE

I could speak for hours about personal style, as it goes hand in hand with my own journey of personal growth and wellbeing.

When we first arrived at Hill House, I came with several suitcases filled with what I now call my 'London clothes'. I have always had a slightly retro 1950s feel to my style, but during my days working on a fashion magazine, I had favoured a look that comprised of slim-fitting pencil skirts paired with heels and retro-styled tweed coats and leather gloves. It was a style that was based on the glamour-abetting use of taxis and public transport in London. I rarely had to walk more than several yards to get anywhere beyond jumping in a car; failing that the ease of hopping on a signature red London bus or a tube was ever-present.

Arriving in Norfolk on a snow-filled January morning put a swift end to the 'running in heels' years of my life. Admittedly, there was (and still is) a lot of driving to be done in the countryside. The joke of a 'country mile' being far longer than a normal mile rings true when you realise that the nearest supermarket is a good 15-minute drive away – and that's even when driving with only fields in view and zero traffic.

Adding a dog to the family only relegates the need for shoes without a firm rubber sole and deep tread even further down the lines of necessity – to the point where my shoes were quickly left cherished, but untouched – exhibit-like in their own wardrobe mausoleum, where I would occasionally stare at them wistfully like priceless pieces of functionless, untouchable art.

So, what is the connection between personal style and wellbeing? Well, due to the realisation that clothes would now need to perform a function beyond being 'in season', I started off my rural life with a vision of what I felt practical country dressing was 'supposed' to be. I was tired and burned out from two decades of working in an industry where, despite popular opinion to the contrary, the main aim was to conform to an image of sartorial excellence, regardless of situation, circumstance or comfort.

I misguidedly believed that country dressing meant the polar opposite of what I had known before, and in my exhaustive state, I defeatedly welcomed the lure of my husband's old jumpers and jeans; the previous house owners' discarded waterproof jackets, some old mud-splattered Wellington boots and hiking boots. This was my regular outfit for a number of years and I must admit that I avoided looking in the mirror for most of them. I also stopped wearing make-up, and was loath to stand out in any way, shape or form. It wasn't due to a fear of or reluctance for my new surroundings – I was truly in love with my new home and the people that I met were generous and welcoming. It was more due to a sense of displacement in my life and career. I suddenly questioned who and what I was; I had lost my sense of direction. The 'Life Map' that we previously discussed was missing, and I found myself floundering in a place that existed at the most extreme opposite of 'wellbeing' that I have ever found myself in. These years I now call 'The Hidden Years', and it's obvious to me as I look back that they were representative of a period of my life when all I wanted to do was retreat and hide from the world.

Any sort of healing takes time and, as I've mentioned, sometimes honing in on our own sources of joy and wellbeing, ones that can hurry the process along, takes time and effort. During those challenging years, I started to document my new life at Hill House and embraced a hitherto undiscovered love of writing and photography. It was due to this newfound sense of purpose and community that I started to unfurl and notice elements of my former, happier self returning again.

During this period and through my own trial and error, I realised that my original idea of traditional rural attire didn't make me feel comfortable or happy. And yet, when I did feel comfortable in what I was wearing – I felt happy too. I discovered that returning to my old habit of wearing bright red lipstick and paying attention to adding a slick of black mascara and a jaunty line of winged eyeliner made looking in the mirror a fun experience again. I had acquired a few more lines, and my face had aged a bit, but the reawakened flickers of joy were unmistakable. Happiness and feeling comfortable in your own skin is at the heart of self-love and wellbeing. Regrettably I had to lose myself for a while to discover that, but there's no need for everyone to go through that process if we learn to associate our personal style with self-care.

Save nothing for 'best' and start living your 'best' life every day.

Of course, living in the environment that I do still requires hardwearing boots, waterproof jackets or coats and practical clothing that will suit the dog walk as well as the farmers' market. However, while I may have found a more relaxed way of living, I have also learned that this doesn't mean that my style needs to be compromised, and neither does yours. We're often told to dress for our body shape, but dressing for the dandy that exists in your mind as well is a far better choice on your route to happiness. I've certainly become a slightly more eccentric dresser as I've started to prioritise my own wellbeing. Choosing your clothes according to convention is too often to please everyone but ourselves. Remember that whatever style you adopt is only surprising the first time people see it. Once you become known for a particular way of dressing, people rarely give it a second thought – what was once eccentric and idiosyncratic simply becomes 'you'. So, as I have regularly mentioned on my Instagram account: wear the dress, enjoy the jewellery, fling on the hat. Save nothing for 'best' and start living your 'best' life every day.

YOUR PERSONAL STYLE CHECKLIST

Take a moment to try on a few clothes and see which ones make you feel the most comfortable. You might be surprised by which items spark joy. I used to assume that wearing a pair of trousers when trying to repair the house and sort out the car would make me feel more comfortable than wearing a dress, and at times that's true; however, I've since realised that, for me, there's nothing easier or more straightforward than throwing on a frock. Apart from wanting to feel nice, it also appeals to the practical side – okay, I'll be honest ... the 'lazier' side of me – that doesn't always want to be searching for numerous items and accessories to create the 'perfect' outfit. Sometimes I simply want to reach for one item of clothing and be off!

Here are a few things to consider:

* If your working life is dictated by a uniform, what clothes can you wear outside work?

* Do you want to differentiate between your work life and home life by wearing something completely different?

* Whose style do you admire and feel inspired by?

While I don't personally endorse copying anyone else's style (purely because there is no better style suited to you than your own individual one), it's nevertheless still very helpful to be inspired by people who dress in a way that looks appealing to you. Create a mood board that is filled with outfits and looks that you love and are drawn to. Sometimes visualising what you like on other people helps you to make choices for yourself.

PRACTICAL OR PRACTICALLY PERFECT?

If you feel better in a dress, then don't be scared about doing supposedly non-dress activities while wearing one. I enjoy gardening in dresses and I'm often asked why. Well, why not? A bit of mud never hurt anybody! Author Vita Sackville-West gardened in tweeds and smartly tailored jackets – and I do that too. In fact, sometimes I look as though I'm off to ride a horse, although the closest I get these days is the manure that feeds my vegetables! However, if you feel great in overalls and dungarees, then you do you. When it comes to fashion, it's all good!

Well, why not?

VINTAGE OR NEW?

If there's one thing that I've learned from the vintage clothing community, it's that our personal style can have a huge effect on our wellbeing and happiness. These ladies and gentlemen positively radiate happiness and pride in the clothing choices that they make. Rarely conventional but always beautiful, there's a lesson to be learned from a community where clothing is a creative outlet, a considered pastime and thought through so intricately and carefully. As Dandy Wellington, one of my favourite vintage fashion Instagrammers says, 'vintage style, not vintage values'.

There are many reasons to be inspired by the details and craftsmanship of vintage clothing, but particularly as a Black woman, there are also some historically unpleasant aspects of these periods that of course should remain in the past (more on race and country house style on page 58)! My preference is for timeless, quality clothes that have a hint of history and an essence of a bygone era. Sometimes it might be genuine vintage, and sometimes it's new with a vintage silhouette. Part of the appeal of vintage clothing is that I like to know where and how my clothes have been made, and that is why I often shop at smaller 'slow-fashion' labels that produce small quantities of garments made from natural materials. It's a personal preference and makes me feel happy about my choices. My clothes will hopefully be with me for years to come – in fact, there's no greater pleasure than when I wear something I've had for 20 years!

COLOUR YOURSELF HAPPY!

The colours that we wear can have an enormous effect on the way that we feel. There are whole industries based on the idea of matching colours to personality types, individual colouring and colour therapy. Personally, I simply go with the hues that I feel drawn to and that I love. There are no particular colour rules in my wardrobe, and as a result there is a bit of a rainbow explosion of shades and tones in there. I might perhaps favour a brown brogue shoe because they go with everything and are extremely comfortable, but apart from that, the more colours the merrier. However, you may be drawn to a particular 'blue' that makes you feel good about yourself. It may be a 'pink' that reminds you of a happy time, a person or a place. Embrace it and wear it. If wearing a particular colour makes you feel happy, then undoubtedly it will make you look good too.

The same goes for the colours that we use in our interiors. You may have heard that certain shades can make a room feel large and spacious (lighter ones) or smaller and more intimate (darker hues). However, did you know that the choice of colour in a room can also have an impact on your mood, stimulating your senses to induce a range of emotions from a sense of calm to feeling happy and cheerful? It's said that yellow and orange make people feel hungry – which makes them perfect for dining rooms. Imagine mixing them with red – known for its ability to induce fervent passion – and you'll have a room that inspires you to feel voraciously hungry at mealtimes, or at least it's a good excuse to indulge! Expert and broadcaster Sophie Robinson runs a colour psychology course aimed at encouraging people to express themselves in their homes by using colours that bring them joy. As she explains, 'Our interiors are a personal expression connecting us to feelings of happiness, contentment and pride. But first you've got to understand who you are!' By this she means taking time to understand and examine how colours affect you personally. This is where the psychology of colour comes in, and it's worth spending a bit of time testing out how each room in your home makes you feel, and researching whether a change might make all the difference to how you view your surroundings.

THE JOY OF GROWING AND CREATING

Growing and creating things from scratch has given me an incredible amount of satisfaction, pleasure and pride. But until I moved to Hill House, I actually wasn't a particularly keen baker or gardener. I had never properly upcycled a piece of furniture on my own and neither had I ever grown much from scratch. I still don't profess to being an expert gardener or a master baker, but I am joyfully enthusiastic at both, enough that I have developed my own 'perfectly imperfect' signature style. Abundant, eclectic, colourful and confident that what I do is always good enough – as long as it brings me joy.

In hindsight, it was therefore perhaps inevitable that at some point I would catch the 'home-grown' bug. I grew up watching my father tend to a vegetable patch, and I distinctly remember him claiming that it had an extremely meditative effect on him. His weekdays were spent in a uniform in his early life and latterly in a pristinely tailored three-piece suit. So, the opportunity to get down and dirty in the mud and cultivate his own tomatoes and dig up his own potatoes had a calming and relaxing effect that helped him to wind down from the stresses of work. It also reminded him of his birthplace, a little island in the Caribbean called Grenada. An island where everyone had grown their own produce and where the lush vegetation provided the perfect growing conditions for would-be farmers on every scale imaginable. From mountain-high plantations to a yard-square patch in the garden, cultivating crops is in the blood of all Grenadians. Even today my now-retired father has mangoes, avocados, oranges and bananas growing in his tropical garden back in Grenada – alongside the potatoes, courgettes (zucchini) and marrows that he learned to love during his many decades living in England.

Of course, not everyone has access to a plot large enough to grow sufficient produce to eat or flowers to cut. But even growing seasonal blooms inside the home can bring immense feelings of satisfaction when time and space are at a premium. It's actually how I started on my journey to growing things and was originally born from the desire to explore simple and natural decorating ideas that would suit my vintage-style home. Keep reading for my suggestions on gardening for any habitat!

FINDING YOUR INNER GARDENER

Garden or windowsill, indoors or outdoors. Wherever you live, flowers are a great place to start if you've never grown anything before – especially indoor bulbs such as paperwhites and hyacinths. You can even grow various small varieties of narcissi that look like miniature daffodils (like paperwhites but the familiar bright yellow), which look lovely clustered together in small pots and containers.

If you like the idea of growing your own vegetables but fear that you don't have enough space, remember that you can grow many varieties of vegetables in containers. The Royal Horticultural Society is the UK's leading gardening charity, and according to their website tomatoes, salad leaves, runner beans, salad onions, beetroot plus many more can all thrive in containers, and are a 'versatile way of growing edible crops … where space is limited'. This resonates with my own experience; in fact, container gardening has become extremely popular in recent years, so much so that there are many helpful books on the subject. (If you're outside the UK, please refer to page 248 for more information.)

If you do have a garden but have a limited amount of time to spend in it, try your hand at 'square-foot gardening'. It's a simple way to create easy-to-manage and undemanding plots with raised beds. It's based around a grid system where various small crops are planted in squares sectioned out by a lattice over the raised bed – making them low maintenance and great for beginners. Another online favourite for me is Huw Richards, who is also the author of the book *Veg in One Bed*, which shows you 'how to grow an abundance of food in

one raised bed, month by month'. It's been my go-to book of choice for my own raised beds and has guided me in straightforward monthly steps.

If you do have a garden but have a limited amount of time to spend in it, try your hand at 'square-foot gardening'.

You could also consider signing up for an allotment plot, or community garden plot, as they are also known. These are plots of land of various sizes that are made available for non-commercial gardening or growing food plants. You will have to pay a small fee to the association or local authority, but they are a great way to start your growing journey – or even keep chickens in some cases. And of course, you will often be surrounded by other enthusiastic growers who may be willing to give you advice and tips.

There is an incredible amount of fulfilment to be found in making a concerted effort to harness joyful moments. By creating a little arsenal of simple pastimes to help draw us out of the darker moments that can periodically enter our lives, we can retain control over our wellbeing and hopefully live more positive and fulfilled lives. It takes a thoughtful alchemy of intentional living, and while there is no single formula for what works for everyone, for me, it's a mixture of making, styling and cooking – all of which I explore in Part 2 of this book.

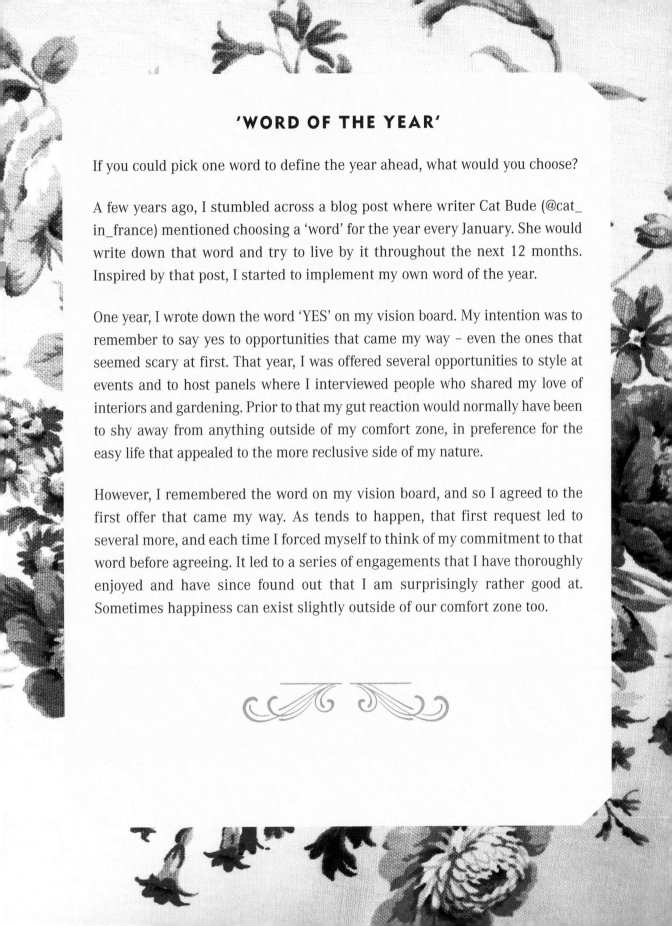

'WORD OF THE YEAR'

If you could pick one word to define the year ahead, what would you choose?

A few years ago, I stumbled across a blog post where writer Cat Bude (@cat_in_france) mentioned choosing a 'word' for the year every January. She would write down that word and try to live by it throughout the next 12 months. Inspired by that post, I started to implement my own word of the year.

One year, I wrote down the word 'YES' on my vision board. My intention was to remember to say yes to opportunities that came my way – even the ones that seemed scary at first. That year, I was offered several opportunities to style at events and to host panels where I interviewed people who shared my love of interiors and gardening. Prior to that my gut reaction would normally have been to shy away from anything outside of my comfort zone, in preference for the easy life that appealed to the more reclusive side of my nature.

However, I remembered the word on my vision board, and so I agreed to the first offer that came my way. As tends to happen, that first request led to several more, and each time I forced myself to think of my commitment to that word before agreeing. It led to a series of engagements that I have thoroughly enjoyed and have since found out that I am surprisingly rather good at. Sometimes happiness can exist slightly outside of our comfort zone too.

CHAPTER 2

Country House Style

The feel of my interiors certainly isn't anything ground-breaking or new. It's a seasoned look that falls under the umbrella term known as 'country house style'. To me and numerous others, this style isn't a trend, but a way of life. Above all, the country house 'look' is about combining casual elegance with lots of comfort. This approach is all about allowing yourself the freedom to experiment and be unconventional.

During the early days of 'courting' my husband, and upon buying a pair of second-hand lamps from a dusty old curiosity shop for our first flat, I was once asked by my faintly alarmed (and now understanding of my quirks) father-in-law, 'What period of interior style are you actually aiming for?' The implication being that, on first glance at my hodgepodge collection of gathered and treasured items, there was no actual cohesive 'period' let alone 'style' to be seen. It's still often the way that an individual item may not seem to make sense to others until it takes its place within an interior scheme – and then may very well ending up looking as though it had always been there.

The feel of my interiors certainly isn't anything ground-breaking or new. It's a seasoned look that falls under the umbrella term known as 'country house style', although to me and numerous others, the country house 'look' isn't a trend, but a way of life, and is the look that I have become known for online, under the moniker of 'Hill House Vintage'.

Hill House is the name of the 1822-built house in Norfolk that we chose to settle in just over a decade ago. A quintessentially Georgian house, it is square, symmetrical and unfussy. It was built for the local brewmaster of a now-defunct maltings, and sits atop a mild incline, which for anyone who knows Norfolk – famous for its flat landscape – is as close to a hill as it gets, in these parts! As the 'Vintage' part of the name 'Hill House Vintage' would suggest, not only do I adore old houses, but I also love to surround myself with old things that invoke a sense of history and tradition. I covet faded fabrics and time-worn surfaces, solid wood furniture that, despite having seen better days, still possesses the beautifully carved shapes and well-crafted elements of their maker's romantic whimsy. I have a soft spot for chipped paint and weathered leather; old and imperfectly executed oil paintings in chunky gold frames; and tarnished metal food domes, goblets and gilt frames.

Icovet faded fabrics and time-worn surfaces, solid wood furniture that, despite having seen better days, still possesses the beautifully carved shapes and well-crafted elements of their maker's romantic whimsy.

As a style choice, this isn't about buying everything on a single shopping trip, but about taking things slowly and steadily and savouring the evolution of a rich tapestry of layers and styles within my home. It's about being relaxed and not too precious – mixing and matching styles, eras, fabrics and colours – but also not being a slave to fashion. (This is, perhaps, a tad ironic, since it was the fashion industry where I first began my career and honed my personal style.) Country house style encompasses many design elements, but the traditional version is usually based around the idea of using items that have been handed down through generations, reused, inherited, repurposed or reimagined, which is possibly a clue as to why the themes surrounding the look are experiencing a re-emergence today, under the new and similarly traditional-values-laden name of 'cottagecore'.

This sense of tradition and repurposing was why it was possible for me to gain inspiration and achieve a similar feel by mixing new with vintage and antique items. One or two investment pieces can sit quite happily alongside a multitude of vintage finds that may have literally cost only a few pounds without ever compromising on style or quality.

The fact that as a design style the country house look can be grand yet simultaneously feel lived-in and comfortable is perhaps what makes it an appealing look to achieve in modern times. My vintage trading friend Louisa, of Sugden and Daughters, calls the look 'elegantly knackered', a term that

I love and which aptly describes our mutual affection for the gently faded, dented and time-worn. Undoubtedly, a timeless look that can be adapted and matured over many years is especially appealing during a period when our thoughts are turning to sustainability, limiting waste and valuing longer-lasting craftsmanship in everything, from our furniture to our clothes, our buildings and household products. Despite an often misguided assumption by many, 'antique' does not necessarily mean 'expensive', but cost aside, what greater testament is there to their value, as well as that of vintage items, than the fact that they ARE antique or vintage and if you're still using them today, then they must therefore have stood the test of time.

I've often been asked what originally drew me to such a quintessentially 'English' look when my roots stem from the Caribbean. In a similar way to my mother, who when she arrived in England from Grenada, a small island in the West Indies, embraced all things chintz (the name for the printed, multicoloured floral fabrics which were popular in the 1980s, but that have been a staple in traditional English country interiors for generations.) It may have seemed an unusual taste for a girl born in Croydon. However, 'country house style' has long held an allure for me, despite growing up at a time when 1980s 'modernity' was de rigueur. While my contemporaries were dreaming of slick and gleaming new-build apartments in yuppie-dominated docklands, I was dreaming of dusty attics, cantilevered staircases and shuttered Georgian windows. While others swooned at the futuristic delights of films such as *Blade Runner,* I peered closely at the set designs of everything Merchant Ivory produced and watched back-to-back episodes of *Miss Marple* and *Midsomer Murders*, simply to catch a glimpse of the classic period properties and their bucolic surroundings.

Thanks to my mother's love of *Country Life,* my design heroes from an early age were the likes of Nancy Lancaster and John Fowler, known for the elegant yet relaxed design of some of England's best-known stately homes. They swept away the stuffiness of their Victorian predecessors by introducing chintz, femininity and colour – all principles I now include in my own interior style.

While others swooned at the futuristic delights of films such as *Blade Runner*, I peered closely at the set designs of everything Merchant Ivory produced and watched back-to-back episodes of *Miss Marple* and *Midsomer Murders*, simply to catch a glimpse of the classic period properties and their bucolic surroundings.

I suppose it could be seen as ironic that the original country house look evolved from several generations of houses inheriting and collecting furniture and objects handed down within families. As the daughter of immigrants who arrived in London without a candlestick to their name, this was not an option for me. My version of this was therefore based around sourcing vintage items and antiques and creating my own country house story as a starting point. Add to that some carefully curated new and contemporary items and my style has evolved to create a home with rooms filled with personality, humour and individuality.

Above all, the country house 'look' is about combining casual elegance with lots of comfort. Contrary to the staid, traditional stereotype attributed to the style, it's about allowing yourself the freedom to experiment and be unconventional.

THE OLD GUARD – THE COUNTRY HOUSE STYLE OF NANCY LANCASTER (1897–1994)

When I painted the tiny sitting room in the first house I ever owned, I used a bold and bright yellow hue that looked gloriously eccentric and cheerful. It may have been an old and exceedingly small railway cottage near East Croydon – some would say as far away from country house origins as you can get – but the choice of colour was a nod to the style and period that I so enjoyed reading about in magazines. If you had asked me then to name the interior designer that had influenced me most, the name that would have leapt from my lips would have been that of Nancy Lancaster – known in design circles for her butter-yellow drawing room above the Colefax & Fowler shop in Avery Row, London (You can see my own version of it on page 56.)

Nancy was once the owner of Colefax & Fowler, the influential British decorating firm widely credited with establishing the country house style. As an American who married into British society, she brought a refreshing injection of American comfort and practicality to grand English country houses, and designed interiors that were made for entertaining and enjoying. These colourful, relaxed and whimsical spaces enabled a sense of grandeur to be mixed with a time-worn yet elegant aesthetic that was personal and comfortable (relatively speaking – when you look at the images today, they are undoubtedly grand!), using a mix of furniture from different historical periods. The spirit of her interior style lives on in every faded chintz fabric, overstuffed cushion and gently ruffle-hemmed chair that we see used in country interiors today, a variation of which can also be found in my present home. One of the best descriptions of Nancy Lancaster's signature style was perhaps provided by her business partner, the equally celebrated John Fowler, who entitled it 'pleasing decay' – which has to be my favourite alternative to my friend Louisa's description of 'elegantly knackered'!

One of the best descriptions of Nancy Lancaster's signature style was perhaps provided by her business partner, the equally celebrated John Fowler, who entitled it 'pleasing decay' – which has to be my favourite alternative to my friend Louisa's description of 'elegantly knackered'!

Above: Nancy Lancaster (1897-1994), née Perkins, at home in 1916.

COUNTRY HOUSE STYLE TODAY

The original lessons of country house style are as relevant today as they were when they were deemed innovative and modern almost 100 years ago. The timeless quality of the beautifully curated but comfortable interiors that are referenced time and time again are still popular today, and this is why the look has rarely fallen out of fashion (minus a few blips over the years).

Above: Our dining room, painted in Nancy Lancaster's signature yellow.

I've always felt that the ultimate aim of curating a well-loved home is to ensure that we're surrounded by things that make the heart skip a little faster, evoking feelings within us that encourage our eyes to linger a little, and cause our mood to shift upwards a fraction, perhaps bringing about feelings of nostalgia and comfort. It's why I personally enjoy a mix of vintage and antiques. I like things to tell a story and have a history – even when that history isn't my own. Of course, excitement can be good too, and this is how the ability to subtly update our surroundings to make them feel fresh and new and not like a 'set piece' comes into play. The intention is to achieve a sense of comfort rather than the look of a costume drama, as delightful as those may be to watch.

> ## Once I've settled on a room scheme that I love and enjoy, it takes a *lot* for me to change things too dramatically.

As a 'slow decorator', I like to take time over my choices and savour the stealth-like 'hunt' for each perfect addition. Once I've settled on a room scheme that I love and enjoy, it takes a *lot* for me to change things too dramatically. However, that doesn't mean to say that I don't relish the thrill of injecting something new from time to time – after all, nothing can compare to those early days of infatuation with something exciting and different.

Contemporary interior designers such as Ben Pentreath, Max Rollitt, Francesca Rowan Plowden and Carlos Garcia are all highly acclaimed for achieving this style in modern-day settings, and in a way that injects the thrill of the new without detracting from the signature style. Today, the idea of country house style means that sticking to one particular look is anathema to its origins, which promoted individuality and eclecticism. Fittingly, there are now numerous examples of what the style constitutes.

RACE AND COUNTRY HOUSE STYLE

As interior design preferences go, one would imagine that English country and vintage interiors, gardens and lifestyle isn't the most controversial or radical of choices for a woman of 51 years of age. However, truth be told, it has recently been the subject of much interest due to the fact that I am a Black woman. As I have previously mentioned, my chosen aesthetic is not a trend or a fad for me, but a genuine way of living and one that comes very naturally to me. It's a style focus born from an authentic love of all things faded, mismatched, vintage and time-weathered. In a world full of chaos, nothing speaks of comfort to me more than surrounding myself with interiors that hint at the relaxed and chintzy elegance of a bygone era. That certainly doesn't sound to me like something that excludes people of colour, but the irony is, of course, that this style reflects an era in which a person with my skin colour would probably not have felt either relaxed, comfortable or welcome.

Despite this, when I first ventured beyond the confines of my reassuringly familiar and quiet life and began to share images of my home and myself, joining a vintage-loving online community that was as equally attracted to that sense of nostalgia, heritage brands and country living as I was, it genuinely did not occur to me that in the eyes of some, it might not be a natural habitat for me. My mother's interest meant it was nothing out of the norm: she was a firm believer that people should live out their dreams and be unafraid of what other people think – so I did just that. (While my mother aspired to the gracious living of English country houses and their inherited aesthetic, she drew the line at my love of second-hand clothing, which in her opinion indicated a downgrade rather than a fashion statement. For her, as with many immigrant parents of the Windrush generation, the aim was to mark progress with new things, having previously been limited to pre-loved by default.)

Another important point to reflect on and challenge is the idea that a certain ethnic group must be a monolith of tastes, styles and ideas.

However, with the mention of older-style country houses there often come thoughts of a colonialist past and a history based on exploitation and suffering. Although Hill House does not have a dark past connected to slavery, it's understandable why these questions sometimes arise, particularly when voiced from across the Atlantic, where houses from certain periods of architecture and location are unmistakably connected to slavery and an era that does not reflect well on its predecessors. In these cases, no amount of architectural appreciation and positivity for the future should allow their truth and origins to be forgotten or glossed over.

Another important point to reflect on and challenge is the idea that a certain ethnic group must be a monolith of tastes, styles and ideas. There is not one 'Black interior style', but a glorious range of Black interiors lovers, with a wide and varied range of tastes, influences and aesthetics. Among many more serious and necessary methods of survival, interpreting style in original and innovative ways is what the diaspora in every geographical locale do best when outside of their ancestral homeland. Some may be directly influenced by their heritage, others perhaps more mildly so, and some not at all. It's all good and it's all just as much a healthy expression of 'self' and individuality as the other. Self-expression at its most creative and comfortable is a beautiful thing to witness, and it's one of my greatest joys to come across a Black digital creator who has put their own distinctive spin on what some would describe as a traditional style.

My recommendations for accounts to follow from both sides of the Atlantic

The stylish Kemi of **@cottagenoir**, who lives in an English country cottage and calls her style 'Afroaristo meets Caribbean nan chic'. Her home is a beautiful mix of the English country traditional with a self-proclaimed modern Black aesthetic; the results are so stylish and in demand that she was encouraged to open an online shop called The Corn Row, where everyone can buy into her chic home edit.

The wonderful Victoria of **@prepfordwife**, who lives a beautifully curated, classic 'preppy' lifestyle in North Carolina, complete with wooden-shuttered house, two dogs and country road trips. Her love of classic stripes, spots and crisp cottons, featuring traditional design elements such as ruffles, box pleats and fresh white wooden and cane furniture is as refreshing as it is elegant.

Some might celebrate their style – as with mine – as 'non-conventional' for people of colour, and particularly for Black people. But what is 'non-conventional' if simply a lack of visibility in a particular space? One of the beauties of social media is that people are realising that certain genres of interior style and fashion are not the domain of one particular race, colour or ethnicity, but the domain of all who choose to express themselves with it – and happily many do.

THE RELEVANCE
OF COTTAGECORE

A close relative of traditional English country house style is the term 'cottagecore'. At the heart of cottagecore lies the desire to live a simplistic and beautiful life, which is completely in harmony with the country house aesthetic values of nostalgia, comfort and 'dishevelled cosiness'. It's in keeping with other beautifully themed and equally as nostalgia-driven aesthetics such as granny-chic, fairycore and the more recently evolving trend of 'cabin core' – something that particularly interests me since I have coincidentally built a cabin as part of my kitchen garden!

What they all have in common is that they suggest a romantic ideal of isolation and staying home, far from the pressures of urban life, which is particularly and understandably appealing in light of the pandemic.

For me, both cottagecore and country house style encompass the desire to enjoy the simpler things in life and find enjoyment in the time-worn and pre-loved. It's a desire to be unfussy and go back to basics and includes everything from upcycling, reusing, gardening and baking, to mending clothes and furniture so that they can be worn and used for years. As much as I love dressing up, I also like a bit of fading and fraying around the edges, and the same goes for my interior style. Of course, due to the turbulent nature of everything that's been going on in the past couple of years, 'cottagecore' was suddenly catapulted into the forefront of the media's attention, in large part because people will always crave a way of escaping the harsher realities of life. I have frequently been mentioned in the same breath as this rising movement. In truth, it has been my way of living for over a decade, and it was only in 2020 that I was labelled as a follower of the 'cottagecore' movement. Before that, I was just 'Paula' being 'Hill House Vintage'!

So, what makes the Hill House Vintage aesthetic relevant to cottagecore? Wikipedia describes the cottagecore movement as 'an internet aesthetic that celebrates a return to traditional skills and crafts such as foraging, baking, and pottery'. It's widely seen as an 'aesthetic inspired by a romanticised interpretation of western agricultural life – centred on ideas around a simpler life and harmony with nature.' Well, it just so happens that Hill House is located in a predominantly agricultural part of the English countryside, which of course ticks a large box relating to cottagecore. However, the adoption of the traditional skills part was a purely coincidental by-product of our new life. When buying new furniture simply wasn't an option, it was time to get inventive, and I started going to car boot sales, vintage markets and auction houses, which naturally led to filling the house with a host of vintage items. Out of necessity, I learned to re-cover seats and make cushions in order to make my gathered items more comfortable and more in keeping with the colours and mood that I liked – all with the help of YouTube videos or a short course here and there. It was all very much a self-taught thing and very much in the spirit of cottagecore – but rather than knowingly taking part in a modern escapist trend, my intention was purely to fill the house.

> W e embarked on this adventure very cheaply, and with amateurish enthusiasm, but with the finished look echoing the feel of an unmistakably established English country house.

We embarked on this adventure very cheaply, and with an amateurish enthusiasm, but with the finished look echoing the feel of an unmistakably established English country house. Similarly to cottagecore, it's meant to look as though each piece has been there for several generations, which played well into my aesthetic since I was buying things that weren't necessarily new but gave the interior a quaintly genteel and often accidentally pastoral feel.

There's nothing quite like an enforced period of time spent away from an unrelentingly hectic work environment to make a person question their life choices.

A major underlying theme of cottagecore is that of environmentalism and a rejection of mass consumerism. It is no surprise that its growth has happened as all of us have been forced to slow down and re-evaluate the focus of our lives. There's nothing quite like an enforced period of time spent away from an unrelentingly hectic work environment to make a person question their life choices. Does your work and lifestyle make you feel enriched and fulfilled? Is the work–life balance that you have conducive to happiness for you and your family? Around the world, I imagine that there have been a lot of tough 'cost/benefit analysis'-style discussions taking place at dinner tables, with regard to what happens when normal life (or something close to it) resumes. However, realising that returning to that fast pace of living doesn't necessarily agree with you has major economic repercussions, and this is why the cottagecore values naturally tie in with attributes that make more sense today than they have for years: self-care, thriftiness, self-sufficiency and slow living – all things that go hand in hand with an economic shift in circumstances. The appeal for many is obvious – a return to traditional ways, even perhaps homesteading and learning traditional but still useful skills, is suddenly attractive, as is a 'make do and mend' philosophy. What started out as a trend has made many people review their life beyond the realms of mere bucolic Instagram aesthetics and prairie dresses.

COUNTRY HOUSE STYLE: SIX RULES FOR THE MODERN HOME

GO FOR COMFORT

'A room should be comfortable, to both the body and the eye, free from too many rules.' Nancy Lancaster

This is what Nancy Lancaster referred to as 'mannered yet casual and unselfconscious'. The most comfortable rooms are free from strict rules and restraints. I remember visiting a relative in New York in the early 1980s. She was an extremely house-proud woman and, in many respects, her home was beautifully presented. However, her sofas and chairs were covered in a rigid clear plastic designed to protect the fabric and cushions underneath. I remember how uncomfortable it was – after initially having almost slid off the seat, I began to slowly feel my bare legs sticking to the plastic of the chair on a sweltering summer afternoon. My father and I spent a rather uncomfortable visit politely holding our drinks – too scared to place them down for fear of reprimand – while our hostess stared at them, terrified that we might scuff her precious seating and side tables through actual use. It was a relief to everyone involved when we had reached a decent enough time period to enable us to politely bid our farewells. I will never know whether she gained any pleasure from her seats. What I do know is that no matter how much we love our chairs, they shouldn't have the power to bring us out in a cold sweat through use!

FUNCTIONALITY MATTERS

There's no point in being obsessed with good taste and trendy design if the room isn't comfortable and functional too.

I'm not a huge fan of the term 'good taste'; it implies that there is only one version of 'taste'. I do enjoy my own style and have a fixed view of how I wish my own interiors to look. However, there are a multitude of alternative styles that

I can admire and appreciate and even love, without them remotely resembling my own. I also agree with the idea that it doesn't matter how beautiful a room looks if it cannot function and be fit for purpose. Our homes must be happy and peaceful enclaves of joy and comfort. They should offer a welcoming bear hug of love – never an icy or cursory kiss – no matter how beautiful.

SCALE IT UP

Scale – the size of furniture and objects in relation to the size of the room – is extremely important.

Nancy Lancaster always believed that oversized items looked far more impressive to a room than undersized ones, which can look a little 'mean' and leave a room feeling a bit unfinished.

I love large sofas that several people can comfortably sit on at once. I also enjoy having at least one statement piece of furniture in a room with which to draw the eye. In my dining room it is a French armoire filled with crockery. In my family room it is a large antique dresser. These are the beautiful larger pieces that we can build the rest of the room around, and they often set the tone for everything else.

UNDERSTATED IS A STATEMENT

Understatement can be good – overdone, matchy-matchy and over-embellished rooms can sometimes be too much.

This may sound rich coming from me – I am the queen of adding a few more cushions and a lot of colour, after all. But this is simply a guide to interpret in your own way. For me this means not trying to hurriedly finish a room in one swift attempt. There's no need to grab matching statement pieces all at once. It's fine for a room to take time, patience and love to be finished. Accessories and soft furnishings can be curated and collected over a period so that you are able to choose individual pieces that you genuinely adore, rather than items that are manufactured to go together. In doing so, you can create an individual style that develops and becomes uniquely yours.

'Keep
Things
Down
to
Earth'

MIX IT UP

The most successful rooms do not stick to a formula. They are not rigid or strict in their period or era. They are an eclectic mix of time and tastes and that is their ultimate beauty.

This is my personal rule, but it does follow one of my favourite quotes from Nancy Lancaster, which says: 'I never think that sticking slavishly to one period is successful; a touch of nostalgia adds charm. One needs light and shade, because if every piece is perfect, the room becomes a museum and is lifeless.' If I could wear this on a t-shirt then I would, as it echoes my sentiments about decorating perfectly. She also mentioned that a room should be like mixing a salad – which is a great analogy.

FURNITURE IS STORYTELLING

Don't be afraid to allow your room and furniture to show its history and to 'show the signs of wear and tear'.

There is nothing more reassuringly satisfying than knowing that at least one piece of furniture in a room has a story. Even if it's relatively recent, it can provide an extra thread to an already rich tapestry. History, depth and substance are beautiful additions to any interior – even ones that seem to be modern on the surface. Similar to the faces of those that we have loved for a long time, the signs of wear and tear add character and life to a room as well as beauty. Although ... I draw the line at dirt!

CHAPTER 3

The Art of Vintage Hunting

The word vintage has its origins in the old French word vendange, *which is derived from the Latin* vindemia (vinum *being 'wine' and* demere *'removal'). It's now linked to the year or place in which wine was produced – perhaps a subliminal reason why I am drawn to the word! It denotes something from the past, of high quality. In particular, something representing the best of its kind.*

I want to share my story with you, and, if you're not already a fan of vintage shopping, give you four reasons that may sway you! ∾

So, what actually is a 'vintage hunter'? And why is the act of hunting so often associated with what the uninitiated among us would simply call 'shopping'?!

Well, the truth is that, in a similar way to a pirate hunting for the cross that marks the hidden treasure, shopping for the perfect vintage items takes time, patience and tenacity. It also calls for an almost obsessively enthusiastic propensity for sifting through a fair bit of nonsense before finally digging up the good stuff! You quickly learn to love spending time looking through a jumble of random items ranging from broken cameras and one-eyed teddy bears, to old baskets, chipped china dishes and brown leather suitcases, and eventually finding something either of truly great worth, or at least, of great worth to you ...

The fact that shops selling vintage are intrinsically selling items of a second-hand nature, that have either been used before or were made a long time ago and perhaps never used at all, means that no two vintage shops can ever be the same. This in itself, together with an ever-evolving turnover of items, means that the potential for finding hidden gold is great. This treasure doesn't have to be worth a huge amount of money, although finds like that do happen, and more often than you might think – but treasure, like beauty, is in the eye of the beholder.

There are many reasons why shopping for vintage items is a good idea. I may be slightly biased – after all, I have the word 'vintage' in my social media name, so it's obvious that the whole ethos of the word is an important core value of mine. I want to share my story with you, and, if you're not already a fan of vintage shopping, give you four reasons that may sway you!

BECOMING HILL HOUSE VINTAGE

It was a strange position in which to suddenly find myself. A self-confessed former workaholic and fashion-loving party girl who was suddenly without a career and had time on her hands, living in a hamlet in rural Norfolk. I was used to being busy and meeting deadlines. I was also used to having the freedom to buy things with my own earnings. I had worked since the age of 12, when I had my first paper round – although my mother would have told you at the time that she completed at least one weekly round in every four on my behalf ... All I can remember is the thrill of receiving my 'pay packet', containing a crisp five-pound note and a few copper coins. Since that first thrill, I worked as a Saturday girl in various shops, eventually graduating from university to embark on my career in fashion. The point here is that I had always enjoyed earning *and* spending my own money.

When we arrived in Norfolk, I no longer had a career or an income to put towards the household, but what I *did* have was a large house to furnish, and an extremely limited budget with which to do so. Of course, we had our much-loved pieces from London, including the Edwardian chair and the Grandmother's Chest, but it was on moving-in day that we realised that apart from beds the sum total of our current furniture would fill just one room of our new abode. I had to think quickly and resourcefully. I didn't want to give my husband or myself any time or reason to manifest regrets about leaving London, and that meant that my main focus was to make sure that the house felt as homely, comfortable and welcoming as quickly as possible.

With our halved income and limited budget, buying from conventional sources was out of the question, so I set about exploring the area for second-hand shops, vintage emporiums and antique shops of a less than salubrious nature – in fact, the dustier the better. Yes, the house needed to be furnished, but as a slow decorator I still only filled the home with things that I loved and was drawn to, some of which were pre-loved! It was during this period that I discovered a passion for auctions and auction houses. Prior to my move to Norfolk, I had felt intimidated and feared that auction houses would be uninvitingly pompous environments, overly grand and rigged to ensure that you would mistakenly bid thousands of pounds on items that you didn't want by accidentally sneezing or coughing. Thankfully, auctions are rarely like the stereotypes that we see in old films. No one will hold you to an accidental bid brought on by a cough. For starters, you need to register before you can bid in the first place, and when you do bid you will have to hold your numbered registration card up high and with purpose before the final hammer comes down. This means that turning up purely to survey the process and have an innocent myth-dispelling recce with regard to what happens during an auction is extremely safe and hazard-free, and something that I would highly recommend that everyone does to familiarise themselves with the process.

When you first begin to frequent vintage shops and antique emporiums, you will probably find yourself drawn to the same type of things. If so, embrace and enjoy it. Particularly as second-hand shops are quite often filled to the rafters with items. Being drawn to particular shapes or colours is part of the process of honing and developing your own unique style. It's about trusting your instincts and being willing to be drawn to the things that appeal to your senses first and your logic later. Sometimes, those things might not be the items that you were originally aiming to source on your hunting trip, but go with your instincts. Explore, pull out a few items, sit them on tables next to other things that you like, and just wait and see if a pattern starts emerging. Often, this is how some of the best collections are started. We may pull out a couple of pieces of blue and white china, and suddenly we notice beautifully shaped blue and white ceramics that we fall in love with everywhere. Before you know it, you have the beginnings of a unique collection of objects that could look stunning on a shelf or in a cabinet in your home.

MY VINTAGE COLLECTION

THE UPCYCLED VINTAGE PROJECT

My first notable piece of vintage furniture was an old Edwardian button-back chair that I saw 20 years ago in the window of an old vintage shop in Clapham, south-west London. I'd always been attracted to the look and shape of this particular style of chair, as others of its type were a regular feature in the country house decor that I'd long admired in the glossy interiors magazines I collected. Unfortunately, the good-quality contemporary versions, listed in the pages of highly esteemed shelter publications such as *House & Garden* and *World of Interiors*, were sold in the prestigious interior designer showrooms of Chelsea for thousands of pounds, and so were not an option. At a time when conveniently priced 'fast furniture' shops such as IKEA reigned supreme for people with my budget, and 'chucking out the chintz' was the war cry of modern, design-savvy homemakers, old vintage shops were left undervalued and unloved places.

I managed to purchase my Victorian button-back chair for about £50, and set about having it reupholstered and covered in a fetching peony check fabric from textile designer Ian Mankin. To this day, that sturdy, red-checked button-back is one of the most asked-about pieces of furniture on my blog and Instagram account. If I had a penny for every time I've been asked where it can be purchased, I'd finally be able to buy one of those designer versions that I'd originally lusted after in the magazines. However, at over 100 years old, my original is unique, still going strong and is now officially defined as an antique, which also means that its value has gone up, proving that good style will always remain enduringly popular as well as a good investment. You just have to be willing to turn a seemingly ugly and tired duckling into a charming swan.

You just have to be willing to turn a seemingly ugly and tired duckling into a charming swan.

That first venture into vintage hunting for household items and furniture was just the beginning of a very long love affair for me. Until that moment when the Edwardian chair caught my eye, I'd always assumed that buying vintage was mainly about clothes and fashion. I'd frequented vintage clothing emporiums such as the now defunct Kensington Market on Kensington High Street as a teenager, sourcing Audrey Hepburn-esque 1950s cocktail dresses and 1960s cigarette pants to wear with Doc Martens. Among the hordes of army surplus rails, I remember seeing the odd (what I now know to be) mid-century modern vase, bowl or ashtray, but never took much notice. It makes my eyes water to imagine those incredibly beautiful and carefully hand-crafted yet overlooked objects d'art that would now be viewed as collectors' items.

THE INHERITED PIECE OF VINTAGE

Having also inherited a large Victorian chest of drawers from my husband's grandmother (known as 'Grandmother's Chest' in a way that makes us giggle whenever it's referenced!) we had unwittingly begun to build up a vintage interior look in our own contemporary way. The chest is a large, six-drawer beast of a thing, which has resided in each of the master bedrooms in all of our homes. It was the first piece of 'brown furniture' that started my love of mixing beautiful old wood with contemporary furniture. My idea of vintage has never been to be totally exclusive to a period of history – I actually enjoy throwing contemporary items into the mix, to create my own idiosyncratic cocktail of periods and styles. As I've mentioned, it's the most basic concept behind country house style – that casually curated gathering of objects and furniture that have been inherited, collected and gathered over time as houses get passed down through generations.

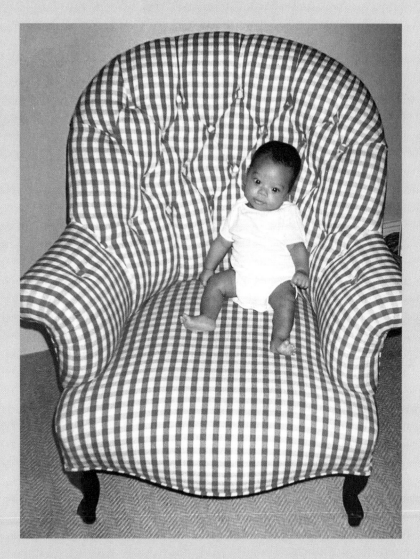

The Victorian button-back chair that I found in a
ratty state, modelled by my three-month-old son
just after it was re-upholstered and re-covered in
Ian Mankin check.

MY FAVOURITE EARLY VINTAGE FIND:
THE CONSTANCE SPRY PLANTERS!

I was drawn the first time that I encountered this pair of beautifully shaped, voluptuous-looking, ceramic indoor planters. The shell-like shape of them was incredibly sensual yet also beautifully classical. Upon finding out that they were £40 for the pair, I bought them instantly, knowing that they would take pride of place above the two large fireplaces in my dining room and drawing room respectively. At the time I didn't know what they were, only that I absolutely adored their unusual shape and wanted to find out more about them.

Therein lies one of the particular joys of vintage hunting: when you buy what you love, there's always the possibility that others will enjoy it too, and the value will rise. But even when that doesn't happen, you're still left with something that you adore.

It was at this time that magazines such as *Homes & Antiques* and *Miller's Antiques* became my reading materials of choice. Once you get the antique-hunting bug, it hits you hard. Having studied art history at school, I had a ready-made thirst for historical knowledge from which to springboard. *Miller's Antiques* is a trusted handbook and price guide to the antiques market. It has earned the reputation of being the book that no dealer, collector or auctioneer should be without, and has become a constant addition to my handbag on jaunts around antique markets and vintage emporiums. Upon further exploration, using the guides and internet searches, I discovered that my large ceramic planters were in fact a rare pair of oversized Constance Spry, Fulham Pottery vases. Constance Spry was a well-known floristry designer of the early twentieth century, responsible for the flowers at Queen Elizabeth II's coronation, no less. (Fun fact: she was also credited with inventing Britain's beloved Coronation Chicken dish!)

After that first sighting, I looked out for more Fulham Pottery wherever I went and was fortunate enough to be able to discover and collect several more 'lost' or forgotten pieces over the years. Usually never more than 20 or so pounds apiece. What has become evident is that my Fulham Pottery vases are now collectors' pieces, and my modest £40 investment now trades hands for around upwards of £700 apiece today. It's a happy accident that something that I genuinely fell in love with and enjoy collecting has become something of worth. Therein lies one of the particular joys of vintage hunting: when you buy what you love, there's always the possibility that others will enjoy it too, and the value will rise. But even when that doesn't happen, you're still left with something that you adore. (See page 96 for more advice on building your own collection.)

Grandmother's Chest in the first house my
husband and I owned together.

CAN VINTAGE BE MIXED WITH MODERN?

It's a question that I am frequently asked by people who love the idea of vintage but are unsure about how and whether they are able to include vintage furniture and accessories in their own interiors. There is often the fear that older items will look out of place in a modern, urban or new-build environment, and that is of course definitely not the case. Mixing styles leads to a wonderfully eclectic look, and the beauty of an eclectic interior is that it gives you the freedom of curating a personal space filled with things that make you happy, spanning any period and style that you want. The cohesive element just has to be *you*!

We've already established that we should always start by buying pieces that we love, regardless of whether those pieces are antique or just a few years old. It's a starting point for any type of shopping that I cannot reiterate enough. Your home is for living and loving, not for show, and that includes antiques and vintage. So what happens when you are drawn to the idea of adding a touch of vintage elements to your interior, but you live in a modern house or apartment and are worried about whether the combination will work?

Whether you wish to stay true to a particular era or would like to try to mix it up, the rules for buying vintage remain exactly the same. Start by looking out for shapes and patterns that you are drawn to and your instinct will lead the way. You might find that you keep coming back to a particular curve or angle that gets repeated in the things that you pick up. For me it's falling in love with the fluid nature of a cabriole or a Queen Anne leg on a piece of furniture, which has an instantly recognisable curve to it with a ball-like foot. I don't necessarily go hunting for the shape, but it appears in most of the items that I choose, which results in a cohesive quality to my mix of furniture, regardless of its age.

What is particularly lovely about modern homes is that they're not bound by any one particular aesthetic and can therefore be as eclectic as you wish. If you're still unsure about where to start, then I would begin with something useful and functional like a dining table, drinks' cabinet, chest of drawers or a sideboard. For instance, my dining table was £50 on eBay, and an old drop-arm Chesterfield sofa was a 99-pence bargain on eBay … the real expense was the delivery! These can all be statement pieces without giving an overly dusty or tired look. Also, remember that you can always repaint, repair and repurpose, so you can have the benefit of a beautiful traditional shape with a modern colour if that's your preference.

Your home is for living and loving, not for show, and that includes antiques and vintage.

You can also update an antique by changing its purpose. A collection of brass candlesticks can look modern clustered together as an installation. Collections of unusual objects framed as art is a modern way to display old items, and modern art in vintage or antique frames is a well-established technique for marrying contemporary with antique.

THE HILL HOUSE GUIDE TO VINTAGE

So why would you want to furnish your house with things that have been pre-loved and previously owned? If you've already made the decision to go down the vintage shopping route with your interiors (or indeed your clothing), where on earth can you find quality items that confirm that second-hand need not mean second choice? Here are my tips for why, where and how to buy vintage.

FOUR REASONS TO GO VINTAGE

UNIQUE AND INDIVIDUAL

If individuality and quirky aesthetics are your preference when it comes to interiors, then shopping for items that are no longer mass-produced, or perhaps were never made in larger quantities, will ensure that your style remains uniquely yours.

SUSTAINABLE

Investing in vintage homewares and antiques, vintage furniture and clothes means that you are helping to keep tonnes of discarded but otherwise perfectly usable and often well-made treasures from landfill. As we as consumers become more aware of the environmental impact of throwaway products, from fast fashion made in vast quantities to cheaply made furniture that isn't built to last, the detrimental impact on the environment is increasingly impossible to ignore.

According to WRAP, one of the world's leading sustainable charities, in the UK alone, consumers throw away an estimated 1.6 tonnes of bulky waste and furniture each year – in the US it's 1,609 pounds of waste per person. Every time we buy something new, we increase our carbon footprint. In fact, it is estimated that buying a new chest of drawers results in a carbon footprint 16 times higher than buying its second-hand equivalent due to the extra resources needed to produce something new. When you're faced with sobering figures like that, it makes sense to at least give vintage hunting a go!

BUILT TO LAST

Why are vintage and antique items even still around and just as beautiful decades later? Well, the answer is that even cheaper vintage has usually been made from natural materials such as wood, metal or stone, which are all materials that last longer than many man-made materials. When you buy antiques and certain vintage, you buy for life. And what can be more satisfying than that?

VALUABLE

New furniture doesn't keep its value in the same way that antiques can. When you buy antiques, you're actually investing in your home with the knowledge that as they keep their appeal and value, you always have the option to resell if you really want to, rather than adding to landfill.

PAULA'S TOP TEN TIPS FOR BUYING VINTAGE

If you're thinking of getting really involved with building a vintage or antiques collection, it might be helpful to get a copy of *Miller's Antiques* in the UK or *Kovels'* in the US for guidelines on price ranges.

SNAP IT

I often take a quick picture on my phone of the areas that I need to fill in my home – whether it be a shelf, a corner or a room. Sometimes it can be hard to visualise the space, colours and shape of an area, especially when overwhelmed by the joy of spotting something you love. There has been many a time when I've pulled back after realising that a particular piece won't actually suit a collection after holding up an image next to it. This takes us neatly on to ...

MEASUREMENTS

Have the measurements of areas and rooms written down on your phone or on a dedicated notepad that you carry with you. Also keep a tape measure in your bag at all times. You never know when you're going to come across the perfect chair, table or mirror, and knowing the measurements of your spaces is invaluable to avoid making unnecessary mistakes.

CHECK HEAVY TEXTILES

Two words: moth infestations! Similar to woodworm in furniture, signs of moth damage on fabrics can be an indication of weakened fabric that is likely to tear or – worse – moth larvae that might stay and ruin other things in your home.

CRACKS BAD, CHIPS WORKABLE

When it comes to vintage china, it's best to steer clear of cracks – even hairline ones. A crack means that there will always be a weak stress point in a ceramic, and unless you're extremely careful, even a small tap will cause it to fall apart. Personally, I don't mind the odd small chip or imperfection in a piece. I quite like the look of a lived-in piece of vintage. I only draw the line if the chip affects the use of an item.

TRUST YOUR EYES

If you're looking for pieces that you love, rather than an investment, then trust your instincts and reach for the things that you're naturally drawn to. 'Vintage' covers many interpretations, so some pieces might only be 10–15 years old and look relatively new. Don't let that put you off if it's something that you love. If you believe that it's beautiful and that it will suit your home style, then go for it.

BE WARY OF ITEMS LABELLED AS 'ANTIQUE'

Antiques are items that can be proven to be 100 years of age and over. There is often a premium to be paid on pieces that have antique value, but unless you're a dedicated collector, it's not always necessary to be distracted by that label. Furniture and ceramics from the 1930s through to the 1960s can be solidly and beautifully made in a similar style to many older pieces. Just make sure that the things you choose are sturdy and the joints are solid.

BEWARE OF WOODWORM

Look out for small woodworm holes and sawdust on wooden furniture. Woodworm is incredibly hard to get rid of, must be treated and can spread to other pieces of furniture – even new pieces. Historic woodworm holes are fine if there's a guarantee that the wood has been treated. Never be afraid to enquire, and if in doubt, it's probably best to walk on by. For this reason, also sit on chairs and press on tables to ensure that they are sturdy and strong.

LOOK OUT FOR SILVER HALLMARKS

Especially on vintage pieces such as napkin rings, cutlery and trays. A silver object that has been sold commercially will usually have been stamped with one or more silver hallmark stamps indicating the purity of the silver, and the mark of the manufacturer or silversmith. These items will usually be heavier and more robust than silver that has been mixed with tin or other non-precious metals. Style will always be a matter of taste, but the hallmark will be a true indication of quality.

CHECK THE FRAME

When buying vintage paintings, try to see how the canvas is attached to the frame. Old nails, aged wood and an uneven or jagged canvas are all indications that a painting is authentically old. This can also apply to vintage mirrors. Watch out for pristine backs where the wood looks brand new and the edges are perfect. It's not always the case, but this can often mean that an item is new and pretending to be vintage. Of course, there's nothing wrong with new if you like the piece, just make sure that you know what you're buying.

10

DON'T OVERLOOK RIPPED FURNITURE

When it comes to seating fabric, sometimes damage is salvageable. If the shape and style of a chair is perfect for what you want, then consider the idea of having it reupholstered or, if it's something straightforward like a drop-in seat, attempt to recover the seat pad yourself with new fabric and a staple gun. Wooden furniture can also be sanded down and repainted to give it a new lease of life (I've done this many times before), especially when the furniture is solid and beautiful in all other aspects.

(There isn't supposed to be a number 11, but you can't possibly go vintage hunting without remembering the most important thing: enjoy the hunt and never be afraid to lift, search and rummage!)

'*Have nothing in your house that you do not know to be useful, or believe to be beautiful*'

WILLIAM MORRIS

BEGIN THE VINTAGE HUNT

I always think that the best shopping experiences occur when the three 'F's come together:

Fate

(SEEING SOMETHING AT THE RIGHT TIME)

Finance

(MONEY IN THE BANK)

Fabulousness

(YOU'VE FALLEN IN LOVE WITH IT)

This is the perfect moment when you are able to make THAT special purchase. However, when buying antique and vintage, you can frequently get away with paying far less than you would for the new equivalent on the high street. When budget is limited, I always head straight for the time-worn and the pre-loved.

Yes, local auction houses, car boot sales, old curiosity shops, vintage emporiums and antique markets became my natural habitats early on during my time at Hill House. However, I have also increasingly bought my vintage and antiques online via sites such as eBay, Etsy and through the many vintage sellers and traders on Instagram (Gumtree and Freecycle are also good options on a budget). When restricted by lockdowns, I bought almost exclusively from shops, traders and websites first introduced to me via social media. Here are a few of my favourite sites to explore:

INSTAGRAM

The best thing about Instagram is the fact that it covers all areas of the world. I have been 'introduced' to traders from as far afield (for me) as Australia, the US and France, among others. You can also use Instagram as a search engine, which makes finding specific items for sale easier, but as many of the accounts also post their own interior styles, you can really discover and explore the styles and items that suit your own home with ease. Equally, if it's simple inspiration that you're after, then there's no better way of exploring your tastes than seeing how other people style things.

ETSY

Etsy is known as an online global marketplace that is filled with cottage-industry makers and creatives who sell their marvellous wares directly to the consumer. I used to think that Etsy was only for handmade artisan products, but in fact there is also an abundance of vintage traders on the website, selling everything from interior accessories to clothing to suit every need.

INDEPENDENT HIGH-STREET SHOPS AND LOCAL ANTIQUE SHOPS

These speak for themselves; they are the traditional standalone stores that have been around for years. Often you will hear about the best ones via word of mouth and particular towns and villages in an area will be known for them. What is particularly lovely about certain types of vintage shops on a high street is that they are often situated in clusters of similar styles of shops. As a result, when you hear about a street or town that has a particularly good store, the likelihood is that there will often be several other similar shops close by, so you can make a day of it.

VINTAGE AND ANTIQUE EMPORIUMS WITH MULTIPLE TRADERS

These are the large – often indoor – market places that have individual market-style stalls of all shapes and sizes selling furniture, soft furnishings and interior accessories. These are some of my favourite places to shop and I can get lost in them for hours. Not only do you get to pick up and hold an item to really see the colours, the textures and the weight, but as each stall is curated and run by a separate individual, you can often see the tastes and personality of the trader quite clearly through their stock. It's quite obvious to see when a particular stall is run by someone trading in Swedish or French antiques, for example, making it far more straightforward to collate and collect items that go together and suit the same genre, especially if it is a certain look that you are after.

VINTAGE MARKETS, COUNTRY BROCANTES, CAR BOOT SALES (OR YARD SALES)

Very similar to the vintage emporiums, these markets tend to have a multitude of vintage sellers. However, they are usually held outside or in specially designed outdoor tents or warehouses. Based on the French style of country brocante (second-hand markets), they are often a veritable Aladdin's cave of secret delights and treasures, and are well worth travelling to, taking a picnic with you and making a day of it. I have often been known to find the most wonderful things hidden under other treasures on my third circuit lap around a market. This type of vintage hunting takes time and patience but can also be a great day out. A similar but less formal way of shopping outdoors is the car boot sale or yard sale, where individuals can sell items in a more casual fashion out of their cars or garages, as the names suggests. Information on these can often be found in your local community paper.

AUCTION HOUSES

The Grand Dames of vintage and antique shopping, auction houses have been around for centuries. They are often an intimidating option for many people who believe that they may be caught out and be forced into accidentally bidding too high on an item. However, this is almost impossible. Placing a bid is rarely a random process and the auctioneers are well practised in knowing when a bidder is seriously committing to buy something or just raising his or her hand to swat away a fly!

EBAY

The original online bidding auction website! There's a lot of talk about not being able to get the same sort of bargains as in the early days of eBay, and while that may be true in general, there are definitely still bargains to be had if you have patience and know what you are looking for. Each trader makes a choice about whether to offer a 'Buy it Now' option. Although you may not always get the lowest price, I do find that 'Buy it Now' purchases can at least give you peace of mind as when you commit to buy, you are likely to get your prize. The downside of entering a bidding auction is that you will never know whether you will be the winning bidder until the very end. My advice? Never celebrate too early. I have been known to be pipped at the post in the last ten seconds of a bidding war!

A FEW TIPS TO HELP YOU WIN AT BIDDING ON EBAY

* Place your highest bid in the closing 15 seconds. Keep calm and bide your time. It's never good to disclose your best offer too early as you will give others time to revise theirs.

* Try bidding with an uneven figure. It's human nature to round off numbers, so let's say an item is likely to sell for around £15 and most people put that in as a bid, if you round it upwards to £15.01, you'll win, purely for that uneven extra penny!

* Always bid up to the reserve price if there is one. Low starting prices will attract more bidders. Your aim is to have as few people to compete with as possible.

* Outsmart the algorithm. The quirky nature of eBay means that some listings may go unspotted due to spelling mistakes. Essentially, eBay is a search engine, so if someone has spelled the phrase 'Original Mona Lisa' as 'Orignal Mone Lise', the treasure can become hidden. There are specialist sites that will trawl eBay looking for potential spelling mistakes. Try 'Fatfingers', 'Goofbid' and 'Baycrazy'.

* Search on 'Last Minute' and 'Zero Bids'. These will look for items that have come close to the end of the auction without any offers. Sometimes things have simply been overlooked so it's worth taking a browse for a last-minute bargain!

* Let a free sniping tool such as Gixen do the last-minute bidding. Take the stress out of watching the bids come in – once signed up you enter an eBay item number and the maximum price that you're willing to pay. The bidding app does the rest on your behalf.

* A word of advice. NEVER give your password to a third-party app or website.

INTERIOR STYLES: A TIMELINE

Now you know where to look and what to look out for. But how do you decipher the various styles and periods? Here is my quick-fire guide on a few of the different style periods that you may stumble across during your vintage hunt.

PRE-TWENTIETH-CENTURY FURNITURE PERIODS OF NOTE

William and Mary
1690–1730

◄ Sturdy straight lines and strong curves. Turned wood, elaborate carving. Cane seats, scrolled backs. Veneering and parquetry inlays. Squat, heavy looking.

Smaller and lighter than William and Mary, often feature the 'cabriole leg', wing-back armchairs. Few embellishments. Space-saving features such as the 'tilt top' table. ►

Queen Anne
1720–1760

Chippendale
1755–1790

◄ English Rococo and neoclassical style. Named for esteemed cabinet maker Thomas Chippendale. Curves, arches, ball and claw feet. Cabriole legs. Upholstered seats, usually a dark-wood finish.

First French Empire under Napoleon. Symmetry, simple lines, in bronze, marble and mahogany. Victory motifs – eagles, bees, laurel crowns, acanthus leaves. ►

Empire (Classical)
1805–1830

◄ Chunkier, heavier pieces of furniture. Large bun feet and turned handles. Elaborate decoration, heavy, ornate, carved details.

Victorian
1830–1850

Based on the medieval gothic period, and a renewed interest in the Church. Ornate carvings and patterns, pointed arches, gargoyles, rosettes, depictions of real and fantasy animals. ►

Gothic Revival
1840–1860

Rococo Revival
1845–1870

◄ Second Empire France, epitomising French grandeur and luxury. Scrolls, curves, tufted upholstery. Cabriole legs, high-relief elaborate carvings, floral motifs, a more 'feminine' look.

TWENTIETH-CENTURY DESIGN STYLES

These are styles that you may have heard of and are more likely to find when hunting for vintage.

ARTS AND CRAFTS
1895–1915

◄ Finishes are natural, 'fumed' (ammonia-fumed oak was a distinctive wood finish of the Arts and Crafts movement, turning the wood a smoky, darker and aged brown in places, which mimicked the antique ageing process of ancient furniture) or painted. Lots of natural materials and traditional techniques. Emphasis on quality, form and function.

Sweeping lines and curves. Very romantic, ► its influence can be found in everything from painting and sculpture to jewellery and metalwork.

Art Nouveau
1896–1914

ART DECO
1920–1945

◄ Straight lines, gentle curves, materials such as veneers, lacquered woods, glass and steel. Cocktail tables with straight, tapered legs. Upholstery is often smooth and vinyl. The Chrysler Building in New York is a wonderful example of Art Deco architecture. Art Deco features in a lot of photography, transport and product design.

Distinctive in that it uses 'new' materials such as ► plastic, moulded laminates and aluminium. Abstract, graphic and Modern shapes with an intentional rejection of historical influence (unlike the Arts and Crafts movement, which looked to the past).

MODERNISM
1940–PRESENT

MID-CENTURY MODERN
1945–1969

◄ An American design movement aligned with Modernism and increasingly popular, it features clean, simple lines with few embellishments.

AN EASY UPCYCLING IDEA TO HELP YOU MIX MODERN AND VINTAGE

If you're reading this, perhaps you're thinking of trying your hand at upcycling. Below is my step-by-step advice on how to re-upholster.

You will need:

* A straight-backed wooden chair with a drop-in seat pad

* A square of fabric that is 15cm (6in) wider and longer than the seat dimensions

* Scissors

* A square of foam padding or wadding that is the same measurements as the seat

* A staple gun

* Dressmaker's pins

You need one vintage wooden chair with a seat loose enough to be pushed out from the surrounding frame. Test a few when you visit a vintage shop or market. They're the ones that look like straight-backed dining chairs, but they won't have upholstered or flat wooden seats. They're generally quite traditional in style and often seen as old-fashioned, so finding them cheaply is quite easy.

Remove the seat and measure the length and width. Add 15cm (6in) to each measurement, then cut your material to size. (The fabric is where you can have fun – use a contemporary pattern and design if you wish.)

For extra comfort, get some padding or wadding from an upholstery shop, or a thin piece of foam cut to fit the drop-in seat. Sometimes the seat will be padded enough, so you only need new fabric.

Cover the seat with the padding, then cover the padding with your fabric, leaving 5cm (2in) overlay all round.

Carefully place your hand in the middle of the seat, keeping both the padding and fabric steady, then gently turn the seat upside down and lay it fabric and padding first on a flat surface. Make sure the padding and fabric is evenly placed so you can still see the overlap fabric coming from under each side. You should now be looking at the underside.

Fold the overlapping fabric onto each side of the upturned seat and pin into the soft underside within the frame to keep it in place. Make sure it's neat and even on all sides (carefully check the other side to make sure the fabric hasn't creased). When you're happy with how the front looks, staple the fabric neatly on all sides, pleating it at the corners and stretching out any bulk. Keep the fabric evenly distributed across the seat and ensure the padding hasn't shifted.

When finished, you should be able to press the seat back into the chair space complete with its new padding. Et voilà!

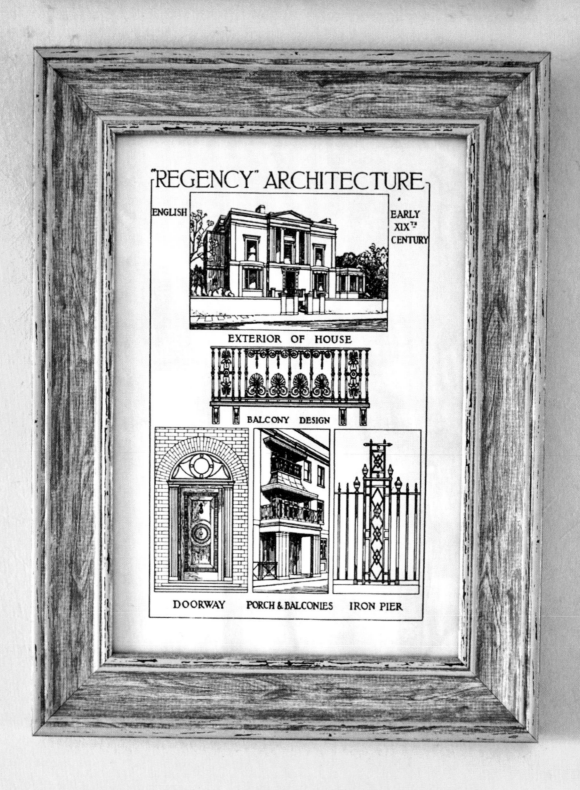

"REGENCY" ARCHITECTURE

ENGLISH

EARLY XIXᵗʰ CENTURY

EXTERIOR OF HOUSE

BALCONY DESIGN

DOORWAY   PORCH & BALCONIES   IRON PIER

PART 2

THE BEAUTY OF LIVING WITH THE SEASONS

Being constantly aware of the weather and discussing it in polite detail with everyone we meet is such a British trait. That said, when was the last time you actually stopped and fully immersed yourself in the weather patterns that announce the changing seasons beyond a few surface comments about the rain? Do you truly notice the changes as they're happening? Do you actively embrace each season as it arrives and morphs phoenix-like into the next? This part of the book is my guide to styling, making and cooking across the seasons.

I remember looking at the night sky as a young child of around seven. I distinctly recall the stars were at their brightest and clearest during the winter months, and how I would tilt my head back to stare up at them from the steps in our front garden while blowing icy cold frost rings into the air with my breath. We lived opposite a large park, and despite being in what is classed as 'urban south London', the winter skies always seemed unobscured and vast in their velvety darkness, while the scattered stars appeared clear and bright and almost close enough to touch.

It is one of my earliest and most joyful memories of fully immersing myself in the stillness of my surroundings and feeling at one with the season. Do you have memories like that? We often have these moments of magical wonder in childhood – but they usually disappear with the onset of maturity, cynicism and world-weariness.

It was really when we arrived in Norfolk that my acute awareness of the weather and seasonal changes began to return, grow and become more finely tuned. Watching a garden that you are responsible for change and develop forces you to keep a keen eye on what is going on outside. If you don't tend to it often, it will become unruly and wild, and although that does have its own charm, it can take over and become all-consuming if you do not keep on top of things.

Learning to fully embrace the elements was a character-building experience, though. As children, we are happy to unselfconsciously splash through muddy puddles and roll about in snow, but as adults we can become reserved and set in our ways, which can often cause a disconnect with our natural surroundings.

The Seasons at Hill House

Hill House itself is surrounded by a circle of mature and established trees and hedges. We have copper beeches with leaves that turn from a rich, deep purple in summer to a fiery copper in autumn. We have horse chestnut trees and holly trees, a yew hedge and box hedging. The main part of the garden can be seen through the frame of the large Georgian windows at the front of the house, giving the view a painting-style quality. It was through the 'picture frame' of these windows that I truly learned to stop and take notice of the magical transformative rotation of seasons that took place throughout each year.

Autumn was my favourite season when I worked in London. Back then it was down to my love of autumn fashion, but nothing could have prepared me for the fiery beauty of an autumn day in my 'new' garden. Particularly on days of bright sunshine with a crisp edge, the trees resemble burning torches when the leaves begin to turn to red, gold and a coppery brown.

Living in an old house and becoming acutely aware of the temperature inside a home induces an extreme need to keep an eye on what is going on outside too. A daily inspection of whether the single-glazed windows are edged with frost becomes an early-morning ritual from November to April each year. Not least because it affects the ability to leave the house to get anywhere on time by car.

Winter is tough, but the upside of a frosty morning is that the icy white coating turns everything into a magical Narnia of crystallised sugar icing, causing every surface to twinkle and sparkle. I have spent every year since that first one marvelling at the beauty of the onset of winter. Country frost is a beast, but a beast with a heart of beauty at its core. Without the warmth of nearby surrounding city buildings to shield and heat the atmosphere, the winter soil is left to harden into slabs of stone. The gravel on the drive becomes as thickly clustered and impossible to separate as rock, and the grass becomes as stiff and as crunchy underfoot as if one were stepping on walnut shells.

Living in an old house and becoming acutely aware of the temperature inside a home induces an extreme need to keep an eye on what is going on outside too.

Spring brings with it a welcome respite from the cold and a joyful lightness to the increasingly longer days. Spring at Hill House has always had the effect of an invigorating fresh shower around the house and garden! Suddenly everything seems upright and awake. The trees look perkier as their leaf buds begin to show. There is a jauntiness to the surrounding wildlife and a glorious kaleidoscope of colours begin to force their way out through the muddy tones of a resistant winter. With that freshness comes a distinct shift in attitude as to where we choose to spend the majority of the day. It was springtime at Hill House that was the catalyst that ignited my - at first hesitant and then more robustly enthusiastic - love of gardening and creating a space that was not only beautiful, but usable and useful all year round.

Summer brings with it the appeal of remaining outdoors for longer periods of time as the rays of a bright but low-amped sun become impossible to ignore. Of course, when one starts to inhabit a space for longer periods of time, it naturally follows that we want to make that space as beautiful as possible.

The second part of this book is my love letter to the seasons regardless of where we live (look out for the flower, cherry pie and hammer and brush symbols to find the different 'styling', 'cooking' and 'making' activities throughout this section). There are many practical reasons for embracing the seasons: spending time outdoors lowers stress levels and boosts creativity as well as our immunity, which in turn can lead to increased longevity. We become acutely aware of the cycle of life and our surroundings. The familiarity of certain events returning time and time again can be a great comfort. By embracing the seasons and learning to anticipate their changes we can make a considered effort to choose activities that can purposefully boost our wellbeing.

By embracing the seasons and learning to anticipate their changes we can make a considered

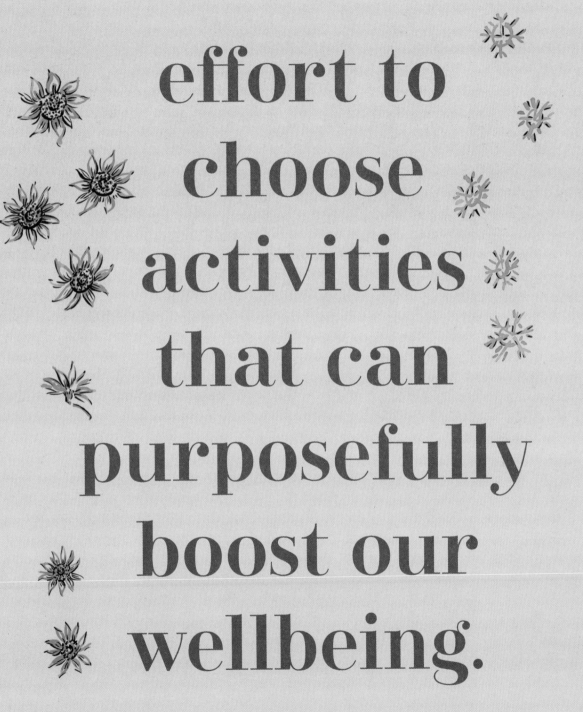

effort to choose activities that can purposefully boost our wellbeing.

Autumn

Autumn is a magical season. A romantic time filled with bonfires, country walks and the last chance to enjoy evenings outdoors before the chill turns too harsh to remain unsheltered for long.

The colours that begin to appear in my garden as autumn establishes itself are an incredible mixture of fiery and burnished browns, golds and reds. The season is a cottagecore lover's dream as it harks back to ideas of comfort and homeliness and celebrating nature's changes through the close association autumn has to agriculture, harvest and self-sufficiency. It is a time when the veg-patch gardeners among us will be stocking up on root vegetables and creating hearty dishes from harvested crops like butternut squash, carrots, cabbage and cauliflower. It is the season where we historically turn from cold dishes towards those that provide warmth, bulk and strength; recipes with added spices and meals that can be kept and stored without losing flavour or intensity, but that can be heated quickly to provide delicious sources of energy as well as comfort.

As we make the slow transition back into interior living after a summer spent outdoors, we begin to enter the 'hygge' part of the seasonal year and are drawn to creating a warm and cosy atmosphere.

The Danes and Norwegians have a word for the mood of cosiness and comfortable conviviality that is induced at this time of the year: hygge (pronounced 'hoo-gah'). As nature begins to slow down and prepare for winter, so do we as humans: calming ourselves with practices that encompass the feelings of wellness and contentment that we associate with being in our own safe space, shielded from the harshest changes that the winter will bring. As we make the gradual transition back into interior living after a summer spent outdoors, we begin to enter the 'hygge' part of the seasonal year and are drawn to creating a warm and cosy atmosphere.

Although we now have the conveniences of year-round out-of-season food availability, meaning our eating habits no longer tend to be dictated by or vary from season to season, there is nevertheless still a huge appeal to embracing the time of year, and to acknowledging the changes that occur in our natural surroundings with our eating, living and thinking behaviours.

Despite the lack of necessity that our ancestors might have felt more keenly, this can still be the season to prepare, to plant seeds that can grow roots and mature in time for the burst of energy and rebirth that comes with spring (both physically and spiritually!). Embracing autumn can ground us and steady our minds, giving us a reason to 'pause' and provide some much-needed respite from our otherwise hectic lives. I know that slowing down to watch the changes that occur during autumn encourages me personally to sit still and take stock of my life at this time each year.

Embracing autumn can ground us and steady our minds, giving us a reason to 'pause' and provide some much-needed respite from our otherwise hectic lives.

This acknowledgement of change can be as subtle or as dramatic as you like. The addition of a few simple styling ideas or perhaps a comforting addition to your mealtime schedule can be the start of as few or as many changes as you wish. Autumn tends to be a slow process. Unlike spring, where the increased energy is exciting and palpable, autumn arrives rather more slowly and is like a clock that is gently winding down.

STYLING

I have always been attracted to using unusual and unlikely vintage items to decorate my home. Creating styled vignettes and displaying collections are two ways of decorating a home that go hand in hand with a love of vintage. As we have previously seen, the vintage hunter is a natural magpie when it comes to collections. If you have followed my advice on buying what you love, and have succumbed to the enjoyment of the process of relaxing into your own individual style, then you may occasionally find yourself drawn to quirky items that you're not 100 per cent sure how to style once you get them home. It's all fair and well deciding to start a collection of beautiful objects and gather the things that you love, but how do you display them to reflect each season from then on?

To help you on your way, here are my top ten styling ideas for
your autumn home.

STOCK UP ON PRODUCE

Autumn is a natural time for gathering and stocking up on produce in
preparation for the harder winter months to come. This is reflected in the
crop harvesting that occurs at this time of the year throughout the country. In
my local area of Norfolk, a distinctly agricultural part of the UK, the harvest
is an important time in the farming calendar and is not only an essential part
of community life but also a time of celebration. Here, the Harvest Festival is
traditionally held on the Sunday nearest the Harvest Moon – the full moon that
occurs closest to the autumn equinox, which normally falls towards the end of
September or early October. The Harvest Festival is probably the closest thing
that the British have to Thanksgiving, and is reflected in many traditional
symbols and events that have taken place for many centuries. It was an event
that I remember celebrating in my own youth at school in distinctly un-rural
south London! Decorating the house with corn dolls – intricate weavings
made out of straw and made to be hung up in traditional farmhouses – was
supposed to represent the goddess of the grain and bring good luck. I still
love to collect vintage baskets and will often have them displayed on top of
cupboards or hanging from hooks. A basket itself can provide an interesting
enough display on its own, but it can also provide a practical vessel with
which to display seasonal produce, or be used as an alternative to vases to
display dried flowers, branches or feathers or other decorative items.

GET ORGANISED

Grouping, pairing and organising by 'families' is a helpful technique that allows you to display your collections in a way that is pleasing to the eye. The look that you want to achieve is neither cluttered nor messy, but casually organised and catalogued. A loose rule is to group objects by colour or by 'family'. So, for instance, during the autumn months, I like to display a grouping of vintage objects and curiosities that take their cue from the colours of nature during this period. I have a small copper camping kettle on a stand, which I place next to an antique perfume bottle that has copper etching, this in turn sits beside a pile of vintage, brown, Victorian collar boxes with the initials embossed in copper plate. On their own, these items may seem a little lost, but as a group guided by an autumnal colour palette, they complement each other. The aim is to never allow your collections to look like lonely trinkets, but to be cohesive and complementary, forming a pleasing vignette that adds interest to a previously unloved surface or corner.

CREATE NATURE-INSPIRED DECORATIONS

Flowers play an important part in my decorating throughout the year, and autumn is no different. However, not all displays have to be floral ones. We've already seen that nature and the natural world is the most dominating force when it comes to styling with the seasons, and so it is with the colour cues that surround us at any given point of the year; in autumn this is brown, orange, gold, red and purple hues. There is also still a lot of green, but the brighter, more vivid colours fade and are replaced by this rich and warmer tonal palette. I forage for branches and berries on my daily walks – sometimes a fallen branch or leafy twig will catch my eye and be tucked into my basket to be brought home to form a large autumnal display. Natural displays do not always have to have flowers – these branches and twigs can have a sculptural beauty of their own.

REUSE YOUR FLOWERS

Of course the seasonal flowers that are around in autumn are beautiful too. Deep burgundy hydrangeas can be cut fresh and then left to dry so that they can be used year round in floral displays. For table settings, scatter flower heads that have been discarded or fallen from garden beds or floral displays for a more unusual yet still pretty and romantic table decoration.

LOVE YOUR GOURDS

Decorating with pumpkins and gourds might not be a new idea when it comes to Halloween, but personally I like to book in my visit to the pumpkin patch as soon as October arrives and call it decorating for autumn! Most of us are

used to decorating our front doors, porches or front steps for Christmas, but there are ample opportunities to impart the same care and styling attention throughout the rest of the year. There is simply nothing more welcoming and jolly than a beautifully decorated entrance, so why limit it to just one season? I display carefully selected groups of pumpkins along with large tubs of chrysanthemums on my doorstep from the end of September until it's time to switch over for Christmas. In order to keep it seasonally decorative and elegant rather than simply 'Halloween-y' I tend to choose paler-coloured pumpkins and gourds in grey-blue, pale primrose and chalky peach hues rather than the more widely used orange. This allows the decoration to distinguish itself from the pantomime theatrics of All Souls' Night. You could also use straw bales, scarecrows and ornamental cabbages.

HAVE AN AUTUMN PICNIC

Autumn marks the beginning of a lowering sun and magnificent sunsets, and there is nothing more magical than a bowl or mug of hot soup in the garden while the last rays of the sun disappear over the horizon. Autumn picnics have a very different feel to the long, lazy ones of summer. They are far less warm for starters, and so the element of ensuring comfort is even more crucial when preparing them. Cardigans, blankets and hot food are a must, and whether you are having a small gathering for two on a park bench, a huddled group of friends on a city balcony or a larger group in a private garden, there are many ways to make your outdoor entertaining ideas a success in the cooler months. Flasks will keep your soups or hot drinks warm. Butter slices of warm bread at home and then wrap in greaseproof paper to keep the slices moist and delicious. Pack everything in a basket and cover with warm tea towels and a blanket – even a covered hot water bottle if you can carry it – and you have the makings of a basic and easy picnic!

SET AN AUTUMN TABLE

Whether I choose to eat outside or indoors, I take my styling lead from the colours that the autumn sunsets provide: rich clarets, golden browns, burnished yellows and copper and bronze tones. These are the colours of autumn and they work just as well inside the home as out. A quick and easy way to reflect the season is to switch up your table dressings to reflect the changing colours that are occurring outside. My style becomes more rustic during autumn, with seasonal textiles such as brown-checked tablecloths and coloured napkins with rustic frills and naive prints in shades of mustard, forest green and burgundy. My green cabbageware works particularly well during this season as green complements the rich berry and brown tones of pumpkins and autumn leaves so nicely. Don't be afraid to fully immerse yourself in all the clichés of seasonal decorating – we should never underestimate the comforting feelings of nostalgia and familiarity that using such items can induce.

·:·8·:·
USE UNUSUAL STYLING ELEMENTS

When I walk around my garden in autumn, I encounter a number of familiar sights that are distinctive to this particular season. Fallen pine cones look gorgeous in large piles and clusters, heaped into bowls or secured in bell jars. Shiny bright conkers that lie littering the drive with their beautiful mahogany coating encased in bright green and spiky coverings. Look out for *Physalis alkekengi* with their immediately recognisable inflated, lantern-like, deep orange calyxes (Chinese lanterns) – another wonderful plant that symbolises autumn and is used in abundance for displays and arrangements. These often grow wild in hedgerows (but will also be supplied by florists) and can be dried to form long-lasting additions to your post-summer decor.

REFLECT THE SEASON WITH TEXTILES

If you are not so keen on the gathering of nature's bounty, then you can at least be influenced by its colours. I have always collected bolts of fabric, offcuts of material and folded piles of vintage quilts, curtains and tablecloths to use in my seasonal styling. In autumn I will look for patterns that have pastoral themes in darker colours, or patterns and shapes that reflect nature. Plaids, checks and leaf patterns work well. These pieces of fabric can be used as a throw to temporarily cover a seat, as a tablecloth or picnic blanket. They can be cut up and made into napkins or an impromptu apron. Most of all, they are just additions that can add colour, variety and interest, all ready to be folded away again and swapped over when the seasons change once more.

DON'T BE AFRAID TO FAKE IT!

Imagine all of the things that we associate with autumn and introduce them into your decor, even if it doesn't make practical sense. You may not have a roaring open fire, but there's nothing wrong with having a few logs in a wire basket near a non-working fireplace. It gives a cosy rustic effect and distinguishes the season from summer.

COOKING

COSY AUTUMNAL RECIPES

As a child growing up in seventies' and eighties' England, autumn was marked by distinctive occasions such as Bonfire Night, or Guy Fawkes Night, the annual commemoration to celebrate the fact that King James I had survived an attempt on his life in 1605. At the time people lit bonfires around London and celebrated the failure of the infamous Gunpowder Plot, of which Guy Fawkes had been a conspirator, to blow up the Houses of Parliament as well as the King.

Bonfire Night brought with it the excitement of large, organised events where communities gathered together to watch firework displays and create huge bonfires, and has been a major part of the British social calendar ever since. Toffee apples (known as candy apples, Stateside) and jacket potatoes wrapped in foil and cooked directly in the glowing embers of a bonfire form a small portion of the traditional fare associated with the event. However, while large community events have remained popular, they have set the tone for more intimate home-based events that can be enjoyed no matter how small or large the gathering.

One of the most distinctive features of events that celebrate the season is the food that we associate with them. It's a predictable fact that our appetite for certain foods begins to awaken and grow depending on the time of year. Whether it's a reaction by association or a need that comes from a physical reaction triggered by a change in the temperature and light, the sudden desire for warming soups, puddings and pies is an association with autumn that I welcome and embrace fully.

CONKIE

A Caribbean recipe that my parents brought with them from Grenada to England and which, for me, shall forever be associated with Bonfire Night was a steamed pumpkin pudding called conkie. Filled with aromatic spices and flavours of pumpkin and coconut, it is a beautiful hybrid of Caribbean flavours (although originally brought from Africa, where it appears in several forms and guises) and the traditional pumpkin-based pudding recipes associated with American Thanksgiving and British autumn puddings.

Conkies are traditionally wrapped in banana leaves before cooking, but my parents always used foil to make parcels that were sealed at the ends.

Serves 6

Ingredients

80g (3oz/½ cup) cornmeal

130g (4½oz/1¼ cup) freshly grated pumpkin (or use canned pumpkin purée)

50g (1¾oz/¼ cup) granulated sugar

100g (3½oz/1 cup) freshly grated coconut

120ml (4fl oz/½ cup) full-fat coconut milk

½ tsp vanilla extract

¼ tsp ground cinnamon

Pinch of ground cloves

¼ tsp grated nutmeg

¼ tsp salt

2 tbsp coconut oil

Put all the ingredients into a large mixing bowl and mix to create a thick, pourable batter.

Create six sachets of foil or banana leaf sealed at the bottom and sides – tight enough so the liquid won't seep out. Bring a large saucepan of water to the boil.

Fill each sachet three-quarters full with the mixture, then fold over the top to create a sealed packet.

Drop each sachet of conkie into the boiling water and cover the pan with a lid, allowing to boil for about 30 minutes. (Or they can be steamed on a rack over a large saucepan of boiling water for about an hour.)

Remove the sachets from the saucepan with a slotted spoon or tongs and unwrap the top of the conkie, being careful not to burn yourself with the steam and heat. It should have formed into a dense pudding-like consistency that can be eaten straight from the foil with a spoon, or unwrapped and eaten from a plate. Enjoy!

CHESTNUT, LEEK & MUSHROOM TART

I will forever associate chestnuts with cosy thoughts of late autumn walks through London and the smell of them being roasted at the side of the road, sold in small paper bags. It's an old-fashioned image – almost Dickensian – and because chestnuts make me think of autumn, they form a part of my retreat into comforting seasonal cooking.

Serves 4 as a starter

Ingredients

For the pastry:

280g (9¾oz/about 2 cups) plain (all-purpose) flour, plus extra for dusting

140g (5oz/10 tbsp) cold butter, diced

For the filling:

1 tbsp butter

2 large leeks, sliced

85g (3oz) roughly chopped chestnuts

280g (9½oz) mushrooms, sliced

2 large eggs

250ml (9fl oz/1 cup) double (heavy) cream

180g (6¼oz/1½ cups) Cheddar cheese, grated

¼ tsp grated nutmeg

Sea salt and freshly ground black pepper

First make the pastry. Put the flour and butter into a bowl and rub together with your fingertips until completely mixed and crumbly. Gradually add just enough cold water (6–8 tablespoons) to bind the mixture into a dough and bring together with your hands. Form into a disc, wrap in cling film and chill for about half an hour.

Roll out the pastry on a lightly floured surface to a circle about 30cm (12in) in diameter. Use to line a 25cm (10in) tart tin, gently draping the pastry into the tin with some overhang. Carefully push the pastry into the tin. Return to the fridge to chill for at least 20 minutes. Preheat the oven to 200°C/180°C fan/400°F/Gas 6.

Lightly prick the base of the tart with a fork, line the pastry case with a large circle of baking paper or foil, then fill with ceramic baking beans, if you have them – if not you can use any dried beans, rice or lentils. Blind-bake (without any filling) for 20 minutes, then remove the paper and beans and continue to cook for 5–10 minutes until golden brown.

Meanwhile, make the filling. Melt the butter in a large pan over a medium heat and gently sauté the leeks for about 5 minutes until soft but not browned. Throw in the chestnuts and

sauté for a minute or two, then add the mushrooms and cook for 5 minutes until the mushrooms are soft. Season to taste with salt and pepper and remove from the heat.

Beat the eggs in a bowl and add the cream. Whisk to combine. Pour the mixture into the leek, mushroom and chestnut filling and stir to combine,

then stir through half the cheese. Pour the filling into the pastry case, sprinkle with the remaining cheese and grate over a little nutmeg.

Bake for 20–25 minutes until golden brown and set. Leave to cool and serve with a side salad.

SWEET TOMATO & ONION RELISH

In my household, we cannot live without a sauce, relish or chutney to accompany everything from cheeses to pies. We traditionally have certain things to go with different dishes, but this relish is a bit of an all-rounder, and is particularly good with the Chestnut, Leek & Mushroom Tart (see page 144).

Makes 1 large jar (725g/25oz/3 cups)

Ingredients

500g (1lb 2oz) ripe and sweet vine tomatoes, roughly chopped

250g (9oz) red onions, sliced

75ml (2½fl oz/1/3 cup) red wine vinegar

120g (4¼oz/½ cup) soft dark brown sugar

1 garlic clove, finely chopped

3 dates, pitted and finely chopped

Pinch of grated nutmeg

Pinch of ground cinnamon

Few sprigs of fresh rosemary, leaves stripped and very finely chopped

Salt and freshly ground black pepper

Put all the ingredients into a large, heavy-based pan, stir well to combine and place over a medium heat.

Bring to the boil, stirring occasionally, then lower the heat and simmer for 25–30 minutes.

Allow to cool slightly, then pour into a sterilised jar. Seal and leave to cool. This will keep in your pantry unopened for three months or for up to two weeks in the fridge once opened.

MAKING

AUTUMN PROJECTS FOR THE COSY SEASON

Marking the change in the seasons is an important part of Hill House living, and the slow change from light to dark as we reach the final quarter of the year inspires many of my autumn projects. The things I make around this time are all about atmosphere, cosiness and making the withdrawal from outside living to time spent indoors as comfortable and as effortless as possible.

CANDLELIGHT IN THE GARDEN

My distinctive garden chandelier, which features in several of my Instagram posts, was the star of one of my first YouTube videos, where I upcycled an abandoned and slightly garish one to create an elegantly lit outside dining area. It was born out of a desire to extend the evening and the possibilities for outdoor entertaining as the nights drew in and the days became shorter. I have always been drawn to the romance of candlelight, and in the absence of access to electricity points in distant parts of the garden, a recycled chandelier, found discarded by previous inhabitants in the basement of Hill House when we moved in, seemed to be the most logical use for something that might otherwise have found its way to a charity shop.

As decadent as it may sound, the garden chandelier is a relatively straightforward accessory to create when styling a cosy outside space, and it adds a little bit of glamour and sparkle to even the smallest of garden spaces. Traditional chandeliers have rather fallen out of fashion for many modern and stylish interiors in favour of more contemporary and energy-efficient light fittings and fixtures. Although I am still a great fan of this type of lighting indoors – particularly over a dining room table – I can thoroughly understand how impractical they can appear, and of course the idea of needing to change not just one but multiple bulbs can present itself as a nuisance too far for many. Since chandeliers were originally made for use with candles, to find and recycle a badly wired, old and battered chandelier at a vintage market or an antiques shop is actually an act of kindness, as it is bringing it back to its original intended use.

It was a simple exercise to remove the old and frayed wiring and unscrew the elements that held the lightbulbs in place. I was then left with the bare shell of a chandelier, which I spray-painted gold and attached to a heavy-duty chain bought from a hardware store (make sure to check weight-bearing information!). This was hung from an extremely solid tree branch and so the perfect candlelit dining area was set up, with the help of a vintage set of French scrolled-metal chairs.

Whether you go the whole way and upcycle a genuine vintage chandelier, or whether you'd rather create your chandelier using lanterns and a metal shepherd's hook, there are a multitude of ways to create a magically lit-up area using salvaged or easy-to-find DIY pieces, so that you can get full use of outdoors before winter fully sets in! Here are a few lighting ideas for you to try in the space that you may have available:

Old candelabras and metal candlesticks are lovely vintage items to hunt down and collect for use in outdoor areas. They are often reasonably priced if found in old junk shops, vintage emporiums and second-hand stores. As you will be using them outside, the condition is not hugely important for that truly

vintage look. As long as the fixtures are able to hold a candle steady then it will create a beautiful ambience when lit in the evening.

Purchase second-hand from sites such as Etsy or eBay if you would rather not upcycle or recycle. There are also a multitude of purpose-made lanterns available on the high street. You will find a version to suit every taste and every budget, and if you are worried about the safety aspect of using real candles, there are many extremely realistic LED and battery-operated candle alternatives on the market these days that provide the perfect alternative to real flames.

Use festoon lights if you are lucky enough to have access to electricity in your chosen garden or balcony area. They make an extremely festive look when hung from trees or against buildings or custom hooks. Equally, electric lanterns, battery-operated lanterns and wall-hung garden lights will all create the perfect ambience for outdoor autumnal get-togethers.

If you don't have an outdoor area of your own …

Collect old jam jars and create little storm lanterns using tea lights (even battery-operated ones) or small candles. These can look particularly pretty in a row down the centre of a decorated table and can be used throughout the year, indoors and outdoors.

Battery-operated fairy lights also make a pretty addition to an evening table or a park picnic. Display them down the middle of the table or put small bunches in clear jars for a magical look, as if the table were lit by the glow of fireflies.

CREATING YOUR COSY READING NOOK

Autumn is all about nesting. Even the wildlife is beginning to think about stocking up for the upcoming colder months. Have you ever seen how busy the squirrels and birds become in autumn? There may be an abundance of berries and hedgerow delights at this time of the year, but you won't see the animals leisurely sitting around and enjoying themselves with their paws behind their heads and their feet up. No, it's a flurry of activity as they pad their branches, drag feathery padding into their burrows, and stock up on food and nuts. They're getting their comfy places ready for the cold – and it's our signal to do the same. Although I do like to be outside in all seasons, I also like to know that when I return indoors, there's a perfectly laid-out spot waiting to cocoon and warm me. My spot of choice is a chair by my bookshelves and a few feet away from a roaring open fire. Make sure that you mark out your perfect spot in your home too. It doesn't have to be a big area – just large enough to sit still, read a book, perhaps do a bit of meditation or journalling or just plain old daydreaming. It's part of your self-care, and it's also an important part of embracing the cosy delights that autumn brings with it. Of course, this may not be possible if you live in a shared rented property. Don't feel it's limited to your choice of space – an important part of feeling cosy is in the things you have with you, as well as the environment you relax in.

CHECKLIST FOR YOUR COSY NESTING SPACE

* **A favourite warm blanket.** Getting cosy is all about staying toasty and warm. You may not have an open fire, but a good-quality blanket reserved for this exact moment of the year will make it feel extra special.

* **A scented candle.** Never underestimate the benefits of smell and calm-inducing aromas. Lavender reduces stress levels and helps you to sleep; ylang ylang is known for its relaxing properties and has been found to aid issues of anxiety, depression and even high blood pressure (although always check with your doctor to treat serious medical issues); lemon and other citrus scents are good for calming stress – they are also said to improve memory!

* **Good-quality socks.** Cashmere if you can, chunky wool if easier. Keeping your extremities covered and warm helps the rest of your body feel warmer too!

* **Your favourite hot drink.** Warm milk is a great addition to your calming routine. Milk contains tryptophan, an amino acid that can make you feel calm, and hot drinks naturally provide comforting feelings. Chamomile and lemon balm are also known for their calming properties if you'd rather not drink milk.

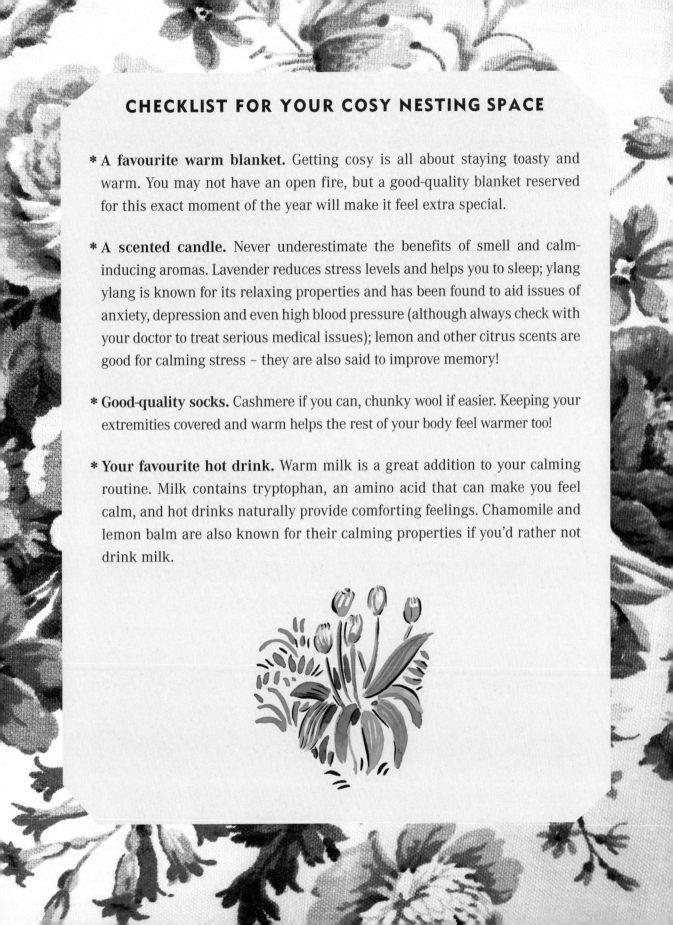

Winter

Winter – the season of cocooning and layering, cosiness and comfort. In days gone by, it was a season that I endured and retreated into. A 'waiting room' of a season where, apart from the intense jollity of Christmas, I spent most of its days with my head down, waiting for the weeks of coldness to pass, and counting the ticking moments of each minute past 4pm in hopeful anticipation of seeing a longed-for extension of daylight hours.

It was in the middle of a bitterly cold January that I first embarked on my own personal journey of self-transformation by moving to Hill House, and a shift in attitude towards the season followed shortly afterwards. At first, slowing down brought with it an enforced acceptance, a realisation that no amount of wishing away would make winter pass any faster and so it would be better to take stock and get creative with my time. These days, the dark evenings and grey skies from December until March inspire a feeling of adventure and new beginnings for me, so it always feels quite apt to embark on small projects during the season of my own rebirth from city mouse to country mouse.

Crisp and frosty winter mornings are incredibly beautiful and atmospheric in their own distinctive way. Invigorating, fresh and certain to put a spring in your step, once you open yourself up to the joys of winter days you will never again see them as the unwelcome gatekeeper of spring. It is the nurturing element of winter that I particularly enjoy. It's all about indulging in the cosy delights of indoor living and creating a welcoming and warm atmosphere in your home. Encouraging a sense of cosiness and wellbeing within Hill House was one of the first challenges that I faced during those chilly first few months, and so I feel well equipped to assist in arming you with a few pointers to help you enjoy the hardest season of the year.

Crisp and frosty winter mornings are incredibly beautiful and atmospheric in their own distinctive way.

When it comes to embracing the seasons and living life the Hill House Vintage way, the word 'cosy' is at the forefront of everything that I do. Yes, there is an incredible amount of beauty to be found around us during wintertime, but ultimately – at least for the life I lead in England, it's the season where I want everything that I come into contact with to feel like a warm hug, and everything that I see around me to cheer me up and make me feel brighter and optimistic, despite the chill.

Living in the countryside with a dog gives me the motivation to get out and about in the fresh air come rain or shine.

However, winter is definitely a season to prepare for in advance, and if there's one thing that the past couple of years have taught me, it's that our homes need to be future-proofed as much as possible to provide wellbeing and happiness throughout the year. You never want to feel ambushed by the bleakness that can come during the colder months, so preparation can be the difference between feeling uninspired, or positive and hopeful.

The days of our homes simply being the place that we lay our hats have long gone. Whether our homes remain our workspaces as well as our leisure and private spaces – now more than ever – our homes need to work hard for us in every season. Our private spots need to be curated and considered in ways that will uphold our feelings of positivity and wellbeing, even on days when we hardly see the sun. It's a well-known fact that the longer the period of daylight, the longer and more intense the feeling of wellbeing, and even if we don't actually suffer from a seasonal affective disorder, dark mornings, shorter days and less light stimulus for the brain can lead to low moods. It's not always easy, but I now realise that part of our journey towards an improved mindset and mood throughout the year is ensuring that we work a few fresh air breaks into our working day, away from our desks. It may sound basic, but it's something that I certainly forgot to do when I worked in an office, and I suggest that you make a considered effort to incorporate it in your winter routine. Living in the countryside with a dog gives me the motivation to get out and about in the fresh air come rain or shine.

There's no such thing as a single fix. But acknowledging that we may need a little help to stay upbeat in winter ensures that small changes go a long way to making life feel more magical and vibrant.

STYLING

Regardless of how big or small our spaces are, whether we own or rent, the colours that surround us, the wallpaper on the walls, the light fittings, the pictures, the textures that touch our bodies, the tastes that enter our mouths – each individual contact with our senses can have a profound effect on us. We therefore owe it to ourselves to make the best of our homes and their surrounding spaces.

One of the best parts of being outside in winter is the moment we retreat to the cosy comfort of our homes. And if you're anything like me, then you'll like the idea of pouring yourself something delicious and warming when the dark evenings begin to draw in. Here are a couple of seasonal projects – including your stocklist for your winter refreshment area.

THE WINTER WARMER BAR CART

A beautifully styled bar cart or bar area is a chic element that was part of my parents' entertaining during festive seasons gone by. In keeping with my love of vintage glamour, I like to go all out with my bar cart styling in the winter months. The festive season is when the traditional 'drinks trolley' or bar area comes into its own, and we can all pretend to be a character from *Mad Men* as we sit sipping from vintage glassware!

Whether you're a fan of mocktails or cocktails, whether you have a bar stocked with every bottle you can imagine or you just stick to the ones that you like, here are a few extras that every bar cart needs – plus a recipe for a classic snowball!

Good ice bucket and tongs

Corkscrew

Jar of maraschino cherries

Cocktail shaker

Jar of olives

Selection of cocktail glasses

Angostura bitters

Cocktail sticks

Lemonade

Stirrer

Lime juice

Bottle stoppers

Tonic water

Cocktail napkins

Tomato juice

Stripy paper straws

Sugar syrup

Lemons and limes

Sugar cubes

CLASSIC SNOWBALL

Makes 1

Ingredients

Ice

1 tbsp lime juice (or lime cordial)

50ml (2fl oz) advocaat
 or homemade eggnog

50ml (2fl oz) sparkling lemonade

1 maraschino cherry and lemon slice,
 to garnish

Fill a cocktail glass with ice, add the
lime juice, pour over the advocaat and
then top up with lemonade, stirring
gently until the outside of the glass
feels cold.

Spear a cocktail stick with a cherry and
a slice of lemon and and rest on the side
of the glass.

(If you're in need of an extra warming
touch, try adding 15ml (½fl oz) brandy.
You're welcome!)

EASY-TO-GROW POTTED BULBS

Winter is a season when there is usually a dearth of floral inspiration and colour. Yes, it's always possible to buy flowers, but they can be expensive to replace on a weekly basis. Small potted bulbs in pretty and unusual vintage vessels can last for weeks, if not months, and can be used to style and decorate indoors as well as outside if you are fortunate enough to have garden or balcony space.

Indoor bulbs will come into bloom weeks ahead of their outdoor counterparts, cheating the seasons and bringing a bit of floral cheer to your home. Introducing natural textures and botanical elements to our decorating is so chic and simple and there's also an incredible amount of satisfaction to be found in seeing potted bulbs that you have nurtured from the smallest shoot yourself. They don't take up much space and can even be grown in pots as small and quirky as a teacup.

PAPERWHITE NARCISSUS

Each bulb produces two to three stems of brilliant white flowers that create stunningly beautiful arrangements. Bulbs sold for indoor growing don't require the same chilling period that outdoor bulbs do and will flower within a matter of weeks. You don't need a special potting soil when growing paperwhites, so they're particularly good for even the most modern interiors, as the bulbs can even be planted in a clear vase or urn filled with gravel.

* Nestle the bulbs in position so that one-third to a half of each bulb is still visible. Don't be afraid to pack them in close together as this will guarantee that the display has more impact.

* Fill the bowl with water so that the base of the bulbs only just touches the water.

* Once the roots appear, you can let the water level drop so that it isn't touching the bulbs. Do watch out as the lanky flower stems on paperwhites can be top heavy, causing them to flop over. To avoid this you can encourage shorter, sturdier stems by watering your bulbs with an alcohol solution (strange but true!) once they've established their roots, usually within a week of planting. Mix one part vodka or gin to seven parts water, drain off the water in the bowl and replace with the mildly alcoholic solution. The alcohol makes it harder for the bulbs to take up water and therefore slows down the leaf and stem growth without affecting the flower size or the longevity of the blooms.

HYACINTHS

Hyacinths are equally as easy to grow indoors and their sweet, heady scent will fill your home with the most beautiful fragrance, making them not only something lovely to look at, but also a natural air freshener! Look for specially prepared bulbs which have been pre-chilled into thinking that winter has already passed. Florists, garden centres and even supermarkets will sell them as soon as autumn is over. Plant the bulbs in vintage containers or specially shaped hyacinth jars, which have an hourglass shape – the pinched-in waist supports the bulb just above the water which sits in the bottom part of the jar. Like paperwhites, they can grow in any planting medium, whether standard potting soil, wet gravel or even water on its own.

* Pour water up to the waist of the jar. Position the bulb so that its base sits just a fraction above the water below. In this way, the bulb has access to moisture without any risk of it rotting. The water will need to be topped up on occasion to stay at this level.

* Pop the jar into a cold, dark place – a refrigerator, cupboard, cellar or even an unheated garage is ideal, and keep it there until roots appear and establish. This usually takes about three weeks, at which point the jar can be moved into a bright, airy room to encourage the flowers to develop.

* Arrange the bulbs in shallow bowls or dishes filled with gravel, pebbles or anything else that holds the bulbs upright. Plant them close together so that they sit side by side without touching. Fill the bowl with water to the base of the bulbs then finish off with a decorative dressing of moss for a rustic look.

AMARYLLIS

If you're feeling particularly adventurous and you're a fan of vibrant colour, amaryllis will be the best choice for you. It is the traditional bulb for Christmas giving, with its larger-than-life trumpet blooms in many bright colours, although red is the most often seen during the festive season.

* Plant the chunky bulbs individually into containers slightly wider than the bulb. Amaryllis need soil to support their roots. Fill the pot with damp potting soil then sit the bulb on top. Now fill in around the bulb to leave a third of it exposed. You can hide the bulb if you prefer, moss is a particularly lovely and natural choice.

* The thick flower stalks don't take long to appear – blooms usually follow on 4–6 weeks from planting.

* Keep the bulbs lightly moist while they settle in, then water more regularly as they start to grow. Once per week is fine.

* Amaryllises always remind me of flowers in the Caribbean, and while they do thrive in a warm room temperature (21°C/70°F), they're absolutely fine in cooler rooms, which happily will also prolong the life of the blooms.

COOKING

SIMPLE PANTRY SUPPERS

I've always felt that the word 'pantry' evokes such homely images of cosy and welcoming country kitchens. The word is derived from the old French term *paneterie* (*pain* being French for bread), so it makes perfect sense for a place that is meant to store everyday commonplace provisions that are useful as well as tasty. Pantry suppers are simply supposed to be recipes that use up everyday ingredients and leftovers that appear in most kitchens and would originally have used home-grown or farmers' market produce. A few of my favourite pantry meals involve the use of basics such as cheese, eggs and vegetables. Pudding rice is another staple ingredient that resides in my pantry, but a fat short grain rice works surprisingly well when it comes to rice pudding, and when I was a child my parents would often make rice pudding with normal short grain rice if they didn't have anything else – as was typical of their 'make do' approach to life.

For hearty food that fills the tummy, warms you up and doesn't take many ingredients to prepare – here are a few of my go-to pantry suppers.

OAT MILK RICE PUDDING

This is such an easy one-pot recipe and is a lovely warm start to a wintery day. You may have realised by now that I tend to add a sprinkling of spice to most things – apart from tasting far better, it's a nod to my parents' origins in Grenada – also known as the Isle of Spice, where nutmeg is the major export and even appears on the national flag! I've used oat milk here, but any dairy or non-dairy milk will do and be just as tasty.

Serves 4

Ingredients

200g (7oz/1 cup) pudding rice (or use short round risotto rice)

1 litre (1¾ pint/4 cups) oat milk

50g (1¾oz/¼ cup) caster (superfine) sugar

Pinch of grated nutmeg

Pinch of ground cinnamon

1 cinnamon stick

Put all of the ingredients into a heavy-based medium-sized pan and place over a medium-low heat.

Cook gently for 25–30 minutes, stirring regularly.

Remove and discard the cinnamon stick, then serve and enjoy. (My parents would have added a few slices of ripe mango to this and you can add fruit, jam or honey too if you wish, but I prefer mine plain.)

PAULA'S EASY LEFTOVERS AND CHEESE SOUFFLÉS

Omelettes are always easy, but the same ingredients can be used to elevate the humble egg to become a glamorous – and surprisingly easy – soufflé.

Serves 4

Ingredients

1 tbsp olive oil

½ small onion, finely chopped

1 garlic clove, grated

2 courgettes (zucchini), coarsely grated (or try other grated veg, such as carrot)

Small handful of finely chopped, cooked bacon bits (optional)

½ tsp sugar

55g (2oz) butter, plus extra for greasing

45g (1½oz/1/3 cup) plain (all-purpose) flour

300ml (10fl oz/1¼ cups) semi-skimmed (2%/low-fat) milk, warmed

100g (3½oz/¾ cup) grated mature Cheddar cheese, plus a little extra for sprinkling

Pinch of grated nutmeg

4 large eggs, separated

Sea salt and freshly ground black pepper

Heat the oil in a large frying pan over medium heat. Add the onion, garlic and courgette and cook for 10 minutes, stirring frequently, until softened but not browned and any liquid has evaporated. Stir through the cooked bacon bits, if using. Add the sugar and season with salt.

Put a baking tray in the oven and preheat it to 180°C/160°C fan/350°F/Gas 4. Lightly grease four individual soufflé dishes with a small knob of butter.

Melt the butter in a pan over a low heat. Add the flour and cook for 30 seconds, stirring continuously with a whisk. Gradually pour in the warm milk, whisking to get rid of any lumps, and bring to the boil, stirring constantly until thickened. Stir in the cheese until melted, then season with nutmeg, salt and pepper. Remove from the heat, transfer to a bowl and leave to cool.

Whisk the egg whites until stiff. Stir the egg yolks into the cooled sauce, then fold in the courgette mixture and then egg whites. Spoon the mixture into the soufflé dishes and sprinkle a little more cheese over the top.

Set the dishes on to the hot baking tray and cook for 30–35 minutes (or about 40 minutes if you are making one large soufflé), until risen and golden brown. Serve immediately with a salad of romaine lettuce and tomatoes.

VICTORIAN PUFF PASTRY PIES

These use a simplified homemade version of puff pastry to form a 'lid' over a delicious spiced fruit filling, although you can also use ready-rolled puff pastry sheets – the end result will be equally as good. The trick to making perfect pastry is to always use chilled fat from the fridge (or the pantry windowsill if you lived in Hill House during the Victorian era!) and ice-cold water.

Serves 4

Ingredients

For the pastry:

250g (9oz/2 cups) plain (all-purpose) flour, plus extra for dusting

½ tsp salt

170g (6oz) chilled butter, cut into small cubes or grated if cold enough (or use equal quantities of butter and lard)

9 tbsp ice-cold water

Beaten egg yolk, to glaze

For the filling:

450g (15oz/3 cups) pitted cherries

225g (8oz/2 cups) fresh cranberries

100g (3½oz/½ cup) granulated sugar

50g (1¾oz/¼ cup) soft dark brown sugar

1 tbsp cornflour (cornstarch)

Pinch of ground cinnamon

Pinch of grated nutmeg

Pinch of ground ginger

Pinch of ground cloves

Zest of 1 orange, plus 1 tbsp juice

Put the flour into a bowl and stir in the salt. Add the chilled butter to the bowl and rub together with your fingertips until the mixture is crumbly with pea-sized pieces of butter (if you are using grated butter you will barely need to do this). Add the iced water a tablespoon at a time, stirring with your hands ideally, but if not then a blunt knife, until a shaggy dough is formed. Add the water gradually – the mixture shouldn't be too sticky.

Turn out the dough on to a floured surface and knead very briefly, just to combine. Roll out into a rectangle about 38cm (15in) long, 1¼cm (½in) thick, then fold the top half down to the middle, and then the bottom half up to the middle and roll again into a rectangle.

After two repeats, wrap the pastry in cling film and chill in the fridge for 30 minutes (this creates nice layers), then repeat the rolling, folding and rolling. Rest in the fridge while you make the filling.

Put all the filling ingredients into a pan with a tablespoon of water and place over a low heat. Bring to a gentle simmer and cook for 10 minutes, stirring occasionally. Remove from the heat and allow to cool. Preheat the oven to 190°C/170°C fan/375°F/Gas 5.

Divide the mixture into four individual pie dishes or ramekins, or if you prefer you can make this as one pie to serve four. Remove the pastry from the fridge and cut into four squares or circles, depending on your dishes. Brush beaten egg yolk on to the inner edge of the ramekins and fix the pastry inside the ramekins, pressing your fingers down along the edges to secure against the side. I like to make a decorative edging by scoring the edge of the pastry with small lines using a blunt knife and sometimes I like to cut the pastry into strips and lay it out in a lattice effect. I also sometimes use a little leftover pastry to create a holly leaf and berry shape to place on top! Brush the top of the pastry with the remaining egg yolk.

Bake for 35–40 minutes until golden brown on top. Serve with a large dollop of thick clotted cream or some pouring cream.

MAKING

WINTER PROJECTS FOR YOUR WELLBEING

There couldn't be a better season to concentrate on wellbeing than during the winter months. A time when not only our skin but also our minds are often left feeling depleted at the end of a long year, it's important to inject an extra bit of tender loving care into our routines and daily rituals. It's not only our bodies that need a mindful and thoughtfully nourishing approach during the colder months, though. We know that the visual delight of seeing flowers helps to enhance our hibernating moods, but with the absence of floral fragrances, as well as a lack of an abundance of colour or the visual variety in nature that comes with other seasons, winter can seem rather bleak. Let's give another of our senses a helping hand.

HOMEMADE WHIPPED BODY BUTTER

In the West Indies women and men grow up knowing the importance of using natural moisturising products such as shea butter and cocoa butter to help with the dry skin that colder weather brings. Over the years I've learned a few simple tips for mixing these 'butters' with a few easily available essential oils

to create simple yet luxurious body butters. On a dark evening a pampering session using one of these can really help to banish the winter blues, as well as leave your body feeling nourished and cared for.

I usually buy 500g tubs of both cocoa and shea butter to last me the whole year. Make sure you're getting pure, raw, unrefined natural and organic butters by going to trusted online suppliers. Cocoa butter has a distinctively sweet scent of its own, but if you want to add a few drops of essential oil, then relaxing lavender or invigorating rosemary would be good additions.

Ingredients

* 42g (1½oz/¼ cup) shea butter

* 42g (1½oz/¼ cup) cocoa butter

* 42g (1½oz/¼ cup) extra virgin coconut oil or sweet almond oil

* Few drops of your favourite essential oil (optional)

Set a heatproof bowl over a pan of barely simmering water, making sure the base of the bowl doesn't touch the water. Add both butters to the bowl and allow to melt.

Remove from the heat and stir in the coconut oil or sweet almond oil, then allow to cool by placing in the freezer for 20 minutes. Add a few drops of essential oil, if you like.

Use a fork to whip up the mixture until it is aerated and softened, then scoop the butter into a jar with a lid. If you find that the creams harden when stored, they can always be softened again by gently heating and adding a bit more oil. Store at room temperature away from direct sunlight for up to six months.

WINTER POT POURRI

Pot pourri is essentially just a mixture of nice-smelling dried ingredients. You can add a drop or two of essential oils if you wish, but sometimes just the natural scent of your gathered ingredients is all that you need. Winter has a very different smell to it than spring or summer. I love the aromas of cinnamon, smoky wood and pine cones in winter – deeper and warmer than the lightness of florals, but it adds to the cosiness nevertheless. You can always buy your potpourri ingredients online and there are many simple kits available out there, but some of these things you may already have in your kitchen cupboards, such as star anise and cinnamon sticks, or can be easily purchased from larger supermarkets. Pine cones, conkers or acorns can be foraged, while rose petals can simply be collected and dried over time.

By creating your own foraged potpourri you can capture the essence of winter (or any other season for that matter) and harness a winter mood enhancer with a personality of its own. Here are a few things to mix together for your unique Winter Pot Pourri recipe:

* **Rose petals.** Whether you're lucky enough to grow or be given roses, or whether you buy them yourself, never toss them away once they start to fade; take off the petals and dry them between sheets of kitchen paper on a radiator. Alternatively, see the slow heat technique for the fruit below.

* **Dried lavender.** This can easily be sourced online, but if you have a lavender bush in your garden or in a pot, simply cut the lavender stalks when the flowers are still buds (they tend to dry faster this way), then tie small bunches together and dry them upside down in a warm place for a few days or more.

* **Fruit slices.** Place thin slices of orange, apple or ginger on a baking tray lined with baking paper and place in a low oven (140°C/120°C fan/280°F/ Gas 1) for three hours until dried out. Make sure they don't burn; if you see them browning, lower the temperature a little.

* Whole spices. Most whole spices, such as cinnamon sticks, cloves and star anise, can be found in good supermarkets.

* Herbs. Pick sprigs of bay leaf and rosemary from your indoor windowsill pots (see page 214), tie in bunches and hang upside down in your kitchen to dry.

* Foraged and gathered items. Look out for pine cones, acorns and horse chestnuts when you're out walking.

When you have all of your dried ingredients, place them in a bowl near a radiator. Add 5-10 drops of essential oils for a stronger smell over time.

Spring

Spring brings with it a personal sense of awakening and positive energy that comes after months of wrapping up warmly and staying safely cocooned with our heads and bodies smothered in warm layers.

It can't be denied that when spring arrives, there's always an extra special zing in my step. Similar to the yellow aconites and daffodils that tentatively poke their heads up as they start to appear on my lawn at the beginning of the year, spring brings with it a personal sense of awakening and positive energy that comes after months of wrapping up warmly and staying safely cocooned with our heads and bodies smothered in warm layers. There's something about feeling the need to peel off layers of clothing bit by bit, like an onion, to suit the changing temperature that causes an involuntary frisson of happiness. It's the only striptease that you're ever likely to witness me indulging in – and a slow-paced, seasonally based and not terribly exciting one at that!

Apart from wishing to feed my bulb-planting obsession, the daily 'what's happening through the window' test is mainly to determine when the first proper meal of the year can be unreservedly enjoyed outdoors. At this time of the year, the examining of the sky and clouds becomes a morning ritual, and rather like the Met Office, I'm not always right, but it's fun to place bets regardless of the outcome. Although I do it year-round, spring is when outdoor eating comes especially into its own. As the weather warms up and the days get longer, it's naturally a far more pleasurable task to find an excuse to eat outdoors and at a more leisurely pace. Once the sun appears and as long as I can throw on a cardigan or jacket and feel comfortable, then I'm outdoors from morning until dusk and enjoying at least one meal in the open air with friends or family – or just the dog – becomes a must. Even if that one meal is a sandwich eaten sitting on the doorstep or perched on a bench located along a scenic walk.

Although I do it year-round, spring is when outdoor eating comes especially into its own.

Flowers and plants have played an important part in helping to strengthen and intensify the sense of wellbeing in each of our seasonal routines, but spring, which according to the meteorological calendar runs from 1 March to 31 May in the northern hemisphere (and naturally at the opposite time of the year for the readers in the southern hemisphere), is one of the easiest times to really take advantage of the bountiful manner of flora that will suddenly be popping up around you.

STYLING

SIMPLE FLORAL IDEAS FOR SPRING

Spring flowers are a welcome addition to pretty much any room. In the UK, they are available in abundance from February onwards from flower shops, supermarkets, garden centres and street markets. Either buy them as cut flowers to go straight into a vase or jug or buy them in pots and decant them into your own vintage vessels for an extra-special individual touch to suit your decor.

Here are some suggestions for how to bring a bit of zing and colour to your home:

* **Daffodils on the bedside table.** Who could fail to start the day with a smile when the first thing you wake up to see is a happy daffodil smiling back at you?

* **Plant daffodils, tulips and muscari in pots and planters.** Whether you already tried the winter flower planting ideas or not, spring has even more to offer with easy-to-grow flowers that will inspire just as much joy, variety and colour to your home. You can attempt to grow them from bulbs if you wish (it's cheaper, but you will have to pot or plant them early, by late autumn). If you're a beginner, make sure that you look out for the more basic packs of bulbs which will usually inform you of the ease with which they can be planted and grown.

* **A welcome entrance.** Don't forget your exterior windowsills, where you can create cheerful window box displays filled with potted flowers. If time is short then pop a few pre-grown flowering plants straight into your window boxes in their original pots. It makes it super-easy to change the display to suit the season by simply lifting the pots out and replacing them with new ones whenever you fancy a different look. You can either keep the plants potted and covered with moss to disguise the pots, or replant properly using a small bag of potting compost. Either way, window boxes don't take up much space and are a pretty way to brighten up the front of a flat or house.

GETTING TO KNOW SPRING FLOWERS

Daffodils compete with the sunflower as the 'happiest' of flowers. There is something about their bright yellow hue – the colour of sunshine – that can melt the heart of even the most colour-averse. If your tastes err on the side of a more minimalist look when it comes to interiors, bunches of one type of flower can look just as simple and modern when placed in a white or clear case. Just make sure that you stick to one colour and the effect will be intense and glorious.

Tulips come in a rainbow of colours, so there is a colour combination to suit everyone's taste. It took me a while to get into the habit of remembering when to plant my tulips for the garden to enable them to bloom happily in spring, but thankfully, if you miss the autumn planting deadline they are in abundance everywhere from flower shops and garden centres to supermarkets and garages. If you do choose to plant as bulbs, they look as good grouped in pots as they do planted in your garden.

Muscari, often known as 'Grape Hyacinth', are small spring-flowering bulbs that grow into sweet little bright blue flowers with tiny clusters of miniature grape-like buds. They look lovely grouped in containers and window boxes but can also be planted straight into your garden borders. If you wish to plant from bulb, plant in the autumn, if not, look out for plants at your garden centre from the end of February onwards.

LAYING A SPRING TABLE

There will always be those who fail to see the point of taking time over table settings, arranging jugs full of flowers and concerning oneself with tea and making cakes. But to my mind it is all part of our daily self-care. Beautiful spaces and calming environments should be the domain of everyone. I may not have all of the answers to save the world, but I can jolly well lay a nice table while thinking about them!

Here are my favourite, easy, spring tablescape ideas.

CHOOSE YOUR COLOUR PALETTE TO SUIT THE SEASON

In spring I use a lot of pastel colours for my table settings and linen but if you don't have a selection of table linen to choose from you don't necessarily need to go out and buy sets in different colours. For example, if I'm using a white tablecloth, I add my seasonal colour of choice by choosing candles, flowers, napkins, placemats and crockery in pastel colours. Use just one colour or a combination of no more than three against a white tablecloth for a light, fresh spring look.

USE UNUSUAL ITEMS FOR PRACTICAL USES

Fake grass table mats may sound odd, but they can create a quirky spring table setting on which to place your plates and cutlery. In fact, table mats can come in all shapes, sizes, colours and textures, but unusual ones can set the theme for a multitude of fun table settings throughout the year.

3

NAPKINS AND NAPKIN RINGS

Look for plain-coloured napkins or gingham napkins in pastel colours for spring. Real linen napkins can be quite expensive, so if you'd rather keep your money for the actual meal, then you can always make your own napkins and customise them. Cut a piece of fabric (cotton or otherwise) about 25–30cm (10–12in) square. If your fabric is fraying you may need to stitch the ends to prevent it from unravelling, but this is usually not necessary – especially if you like to keep things rustic, like I do! You can add extra colour by using ribbons as a napkin ring, and for an extra spring touch, push a small flower stem – such as a daisy or a small rose bud, or even a sprig of rosemary through your ring for decoration.

WHIMSICAL TOUCHES ARE ALWAYS FUN

These can be decoration purely for decoration's sake – such as flocked rabbits to sit down the middle of your table. (Many shops do a huge range of Easter-themed table decorations in time for spring.) Or place pastel-coloured eggs or flowers in the middle of the plate pre-dinner as decoration.

KEEP A TABLE-SETTING BASKET

I keep a basket full of props to add a touch of whimsy to my table settings. These might include hat boxes and cake stands, copper kettles and decorative tins, or vintage glass bowls full of sweets and treats. It looks pretty and interesting, and if it fits in with a theme or colour scheme then I'll use it!

HAVE FUN WITH NAME CARDS

You can customise each place setting with an individual name card. These can be as simple as a handwritten name on card, or something more imaginative such as a name on an egg in an eggcup. A Polaroid picture of a different flower in each place is a sweet idea, or perhaps a single flower in a bud vase with a label. Throughout the year you can adjust this to suit the seasons – for instance, a name on a large festive bauble in December or on a mini pumpkin in autumn.

CHOOSE YOUR TABLEWARE WITH COLOUR IN MIND

It's a well-known fact that I am something of a china addict, with cupboards full of both vintage and new crockery. It doesn't necessarily have to be an expensive pursuit either. Large dining sets have fallen out of fashion, but what this does mean is that nice vintage sets can be easily found in vintage shops and markets for much lower prices than their equivalents in department stores – often complete with gravy boats and matching tureens.

LOOK OUT FOR INTERESTING COLOURS AND STRONG SHAPES

One of my favourite designs is cabbageware, which is always a winner for use during spring due to its gorgeous green colour and organic shapes.

LOOK FOR PATTERNS WITH PINKS, LIGHT BLUES AND YELLOWS TOO

All of these colours work beautifully for spring, but above all, buy the colours and things that you love.

GO LARGE WITH YOUR CENTREPIECE

Flowers are the easiest way to dress up a dining table for the season, and having a centrepiece makes even the smallest table set for two seem special. If your table is long and narrow, you can try putting several bud vases with a tulip in each one along the length of it, but if your table is nice and wide, then your centrepiece can consist of a larger floral arrangement, ornaments (remember those flocked rabbits!), painted Easter eggs, jugs full of flowers or a cake stand covered in decorations – or cakes! For a simple, calming idea, try filling small bowls with water and placing cut flower heads inside for a pretty floating effect.

DON'T FORGET YOUR CANDLES

Candles can adorn your table placed in traditional candlesticks and candelabra, but failing that, you can place them in jam jars, clean and empty tin cans – even egg cups. Wide pillar candles can simply be placed in saucers or directly on to a metal or wooden table if you're happy for the wax to fall. Candles will always add atmosphere and romance, so they are the perfect addition to a dining table – just be careful with flames and ensure that they are away from children and cannot topple over. Lanterns and hurricane jars or tea lights in jam jars are a great idea for that very reason.

COOKING

SIMPLE SPRING RECIPES FOR LIGHT ENTERTAINING

When the moment comes for me to fling open my doors and start using the garden properly again, it's time to think about socialising with a few friends and making easy recipes that can feed several people without taking too much energy or fuss. In my opinion everyone enjoys a perfectly imperfect sponge cake, and vintage platters or wooden boards filled with gathered feasts are particularly quick and easy to put together.

VICTORIA SPONGE CAKE WITH CREAM

I'm known for my – as I like to call them – 'perfectly imperfect' cakes. Layered sponge cakes sandwiched with all manner of delightful fillings including buttercream icing, but particularly fresh whipped cream and fruits and jam. I also like to add cinnamon and nutmeg to the sponge as it reminds me of my mother's baking, but they're not essential – vanilla extract on its own is still delicious!

I very rarely follow a strict recipe when baking – my mantra is 'the same weight (in ounces) of butter, sugar, flour and half as many eggs'. So, for example, if I were making 12 cupcakes I would use 225g (8oz) each of butter, sugar and flour and then 4 eggs; for a single-layer sponge, it would be 175g (6oz) of butter, sugar, flour and 3 eggs. This means that I can whip up quick batches of things wherever I am without having to check recipes.

Makes 1 large cake – two tiers, but when I'm feeling extravagant, I like to double it, to make a four-tiered perfectly decadent whopper!

Ingredients

For the cake:

340g (12oz) softened butter

340g (12oz/1½ cups plus 1 tbsp) caster (superfine) sugar

6 eggs, beaten

1 tsp vanilla extract

½ tsp baking powder

½ tsp ground cinnamon

½ tsp grated nutmeg

340g (12oz/scant 2¾ cups) self-raising flour, plus extra for dusting

¼ tsp fine salt

For the filling:

500ml (18fl oz/2 cups) whipping cream

1½ tbsp icing (confectioner's) sugar, plus extra for dusting (optional)

Strawberry jam (jelly) or fruit of your choice – I also use fig, raspberry or blueberry jam, or lemon curd

400g (14oz) strawberries, sliced

250g (9oz) raspberries

Preheat the oven to 180°C/160°C fan/350°F/Gas 4 and grease and line three 20cm (8in) cake tins with non-stick baking paper and dust with flour.

In a large bowl, beat together the butter and sugar until pale and creamy. Add the eggs and vanilla extract and stir in.

Add the baking powder, cinnamon and nutmeg to the flour and stir to combine. Sift in half the flour and fold in with a spoon. Repeat with the remaining flour until you have a smooth batter, then share evenly into the prepared tins.

Bake in the centre of the oven for 25–30 minutes, or until a skewer inserted in the middle comes out clean. Remove from the oven, cool in the tins for 10 minutes, then transfer to a wire rack to cool completely.

For the filling, pour the cream into a bowl, add the sugar and use a hand-held electric whisk to whip to soft peaks (or beat by hand for a major workout!).

Once the sponges have cooled, place the bottom tier on a cake stand. Spread with a layer of jam, then dollop two generous spoonfuls of the cream on top and spread so that it reaches the edges. Sprinkle sliced strawberries and whole raspberries on top of the cream, making sure that some are at the edge of the sponge so that they can peek out prettily when you cover them with the next layer. Place another layer of sponge on top – for this final layer, do not spread the top with jam – simply finish with whipped cream or dust with icing sugar, and pop on whole strawberries and raspberries.

Use a long knife and cake spatula for serving with a nice cup of tea. Enjoy!

EASY CHEESE & CHARCUTERIE DISPLAY BOARD

Anything that can elevate a simple meal to something rather more stylish and beautifully presented is fine by me, and charcuterie boards are a must-have when it comes to easy yet stylish snacks and suppers. At the end of the day, a good charcuterie board of prepared meats or a simple cheese board is nothing but pre-prepared food on a large platter.

The board can be filled with cured meats with the addition of cheese, olives, vegetables, nuts, dried fruits, crackers and cheese. It can also include ingredients and relishes that will complement the meats and cheese, such as fig jams and onion relish. I also like to use fruit such as grapes, cherries and fresh figs and melon, plus dried fruit such as apricots, figs and dates. With a few clever styling ideas and a great combination of edible delights, you can wow your guest(s) into feeling as though you've spent hours preparing a feast, allowing you to be a generous host or hostess with minimum effort. Here are my suggestions for what to include:

Cured meats. Have a selection of items such as salami, pâté, ham, sausages, Parma ham and prosciutto. Or even a rustic sausagemeat pie, sliced and portioned out, ready to serve.

Crackers and bread. Add small dishes of crackers, a basket with sliced baguettes or bread rolls and vintage jugs filled with breadsticks to accompany your boards. Don't forget to have a butter dish if you are serving bread.

Cheese. If you're adding cheese to a charcuterie board, remember to add a little something to suit all tastes. Hard cheeses like Cheddar, Parmesan and Gruyère sit nicely alongside softer cheeses like Brie or Camembert. You can then throw in something more unusual or a little stronger, such as a blue cheese like gorgonzola or English Shropshire Blue.

Pickles. A few small bowls filled with pickles and gherkins is always a lovely addition to a charcuterie board. Their sharpness and acidity will cut through the richness of the cured meats and cheese.

Jams, relishes and preserves. The sticky sweetness of these three are a delicious contrast to the savoury meats and cheese and are an essential accompaniment to your board.

Nuts. Either create little piles nestled on the board itself or fill mini bowls with pistachios, pecans, salted almonds

and macadamia nuts. (As nut allergies can be serious, make sure you survey attendees for any allergies and keep separate containers!)

Fresh fruit. Sliced pears and apples, figs, pomegranates, raspberries, blackberries and bunches of grapes all look wonderful on boards, but also add a fresh palette-cleansing tartness against the meat and cheeses.

Olives. These make a lovely natural accompaniment to cheese in all shapes and forms. Try black, green, stuffed, chilli and pimento.

Now you've decided what to serve, it's time to think about how to present everything. Here are some ideas for adding a bit of extra style and glamour to your display:

The serving dish. The vessel on which you serve your charcuterie or cheese can make all the difference to the overall presentation and feel of your meal. I have two particular types of serving dish, depending on the type of evening. For an at-home, casual affair, I use large wooden chopping boards. They give a more rustic look, and when they are very large, the expanse of wood adds to the authentic drama and brings a casual charm. If I am having a more serious and elegant affair, then I will use a vintage china serving platter instead. This gives a more elegant French vintage look and can be very chic. Alternative ideas are marble chopping boards and slate boards. Or you can use mini slate boards for a charming way to serve individual portions so that everyone has their own charcuterie board.

Themed foods. As you can see, there are so many options for what to include, but you can narrow these down by theming your charcuterie or cheese board to include meats and cheeses from just one region. For instance, you could choose an Italian theme and have mini mozzarella balls, Parmesan cheese, salami, Parma ham, sun-dried tomatoes and olives with small squares of focaccia bread or crostini on the side. For a French feel, try a selection of French cheeses such as Brie and Camembert and a strong blue cheese, then add pâté and cornichons, some saucisson sec and some soft French hams, red grapes and mustard. For a Middle Eastern-style platter, try adding hummus, pomegranates, honey, dried figs, dates, vine leaves stuffed with rice, sliced pitta bread, hard cheeses and olives.

Annotate. The current trend for extravagant charcuterie platters has everything piled up against everything else. It makes for an incredibly beautiful and very dramatic look. However, in order for your guests not to miss out on anything, why not have a few mini flags with handwritten indicators of what lies beneath. If nothing else, it will help stop you being asked what everything is while you're entertaining your guests with sparkling conversation elsewhere!

Utensils. If you want to be extra fancy don't forget to add mini butter knives and cocktail forks, if you have them, and also a pile of small plates and napkins.

Present all of these items in vintage bowls and jars for added effect. Cutlery always looks great in creamery jugs or ceramic jars, and square paper napkins are lovely piled up in a small basket or on top of a pretty plate.

MAKING

A TRIBUTE TO SPRING FLOWERS

As you have seen, I love to introduce flowers into my decorating throughout the year, but spring is when the idea of floral decorating really comes into its own. Whether it's the sudden appearance of snowdrops and crocuses on grassy roadside verges or bright yellow daffodils peeping up through the lawn in my own garden, there is something about the steady appearance of spring sunshine coinciding with these wild and free floral displays that makes me see '*La vie en rose!*' Here are a few projects to help you view the season that way too!

SPRING WREATH

Although I often make my own wreath frames from scratch using long twigs and light branches from my garden, I do also buy pre-made frames from florist shops and online. When buying ready-made frames, there are two types that I use, the more natural type, made from natural vine or rattan formed into a circle, is perfect for a more rustic look. The other type of wreath base is made from a sturdy wire-ring frame and is ideal for incorporating anything from fresh and dried flowers to berries, leaves, feathers and pretty much whatever else you want to stick in there. To keep it rustic and natural, I use organic materials and real flowers, however, you can just as easily attach Christmas baubles, faux Easter eggs and ribbons to create your own seasonal combination.

You will need:

* **Wreath frame** – natural or wire.

* **Florist wire** – this is a green-coated thin but hardy wire. Use to wrap around flower stems and pierce through leaves, ribbons and feathers, which you can then attach by wrapping the other end on to the wreath.

* **Glue gun** – these aren't strictly essential as the wire can secure most things, however, they are good for adding decorative elements such as baubles, pine cones, dried flowers, bows and other motifs.

* **Ribbon** – I keep and collect ribbons from packaging, presents, hair accessories and soft furnishings. I'm a bit of a magpie when it comes to hoarding pretty things, but they always come in handy for various craft pursuits and I highly recommend you start doing this too – don't send it to landfill!

* **A selection of flowers, baubles, feathers, leaves, etc.**

* **Moss** – this can be useful to pad out your wreath base.

Seasonal wreath combination ideas

Spring – daffodils, tulips and muscari.

Summer – lavender, roses, white heather, sunflower heads, dried wheat, dried flowers.

Winter/Christmas – lots of holly, dried oranges, pine cones, eucalyptus, bay leaves and even faux apples.

Autumn – dried and faded hydrangea heads, autumnal-hued leaves, miniature gourds/pumpkins, rosemary branches, berries on twigs.

Start by laying out your decorations and embellishments on a flat table or the floor to evenly surround your wreath. It's always best to do this before you actually start attaching anything to the wreath, to make sure that you are happy with the layout.

Cut your florist wire into lengths of about 5–8cm (2–3in) and use to pierce the ends of your flower stems or twist around your twigs, feathers and dried flowers. Once attached to your flower, simply bend the wire so that it looks like a hair grip and attach to your wreath frame, pushing the sharp ends into the natural wreath or twisting the piece around the wire frame.

Keep building and adding until you reach your desired fullness and depth.

HOMEGROWN HERBS IN VINTAGE POTS

We might not all be gourmet cooks or have a vast knowledge of culinary expertise, but we can all take steps to being better-equipped home chefs by using fresh herbs in our cooking. Whether it's coriander (cilantro) leaves to add to an omelette, basil leaves mixed in with a tomato and mozzarella salad or chopped parsley to sprinkle over buttered new potatoes, fresh herbs add an element of extra flavour to any dish, and when you grow them yourself there's the added benefit of personal pride and satisfaction, which in my view makes everything taste better! Growing fresh herbs from seed in your own kitchen garden is the ultimate dream, however, you don't need tonnes of space to grow herbs – in fact you can create your essential herb 'garden' on a shelf in your kitchen by starting off with grow-your-own seed kits or even readily available fresh herb tubs from your local supermarket or farmers' markets.

Growing herbs from seeds isn't as difficult as it sounds. You just really only need sunlight (probably about 5–6 hours per day, if possible, so on a windowsill is perfect), small containers that have drainage (I use vintage containers as the attractive surround, but often keep the actual herbs in plastic pots or liners so that they can be watered without being bogged down by excess water), some potting soil, some liquid fertiliser and a few seeds. The seed packets will tell you how each herb likes to be situated, for example, basil likes a lot of sun and warmth, so is best kept in a south-facing window. Parsley and thyme also like full sun but will also grow in an east- or west-facing window – albeit at a far slower rate. It may be a bit of trial and error, but you'll soon work out which herbs like to live where, and the satisfaction gained from seeing your sprouts begin to appear is almost as good as eventually eating your herbs further down the growth cycle.

If you'd rather not have lots of individual pots, then planting a selection of herbs in one strawberry pot may be another idea for you. A classic strawberry pot is an upright terracotta planter which has been specially designed for growing strawberries. It features multiple planting holes that allow the fruit to cascade down the sides, creating a beautiful and decorative display. This makes them the perfect vessels for separating and growing different herbs in one pot. As a strawberry pot is larger than your average small flower pot, this can go on a doorstep, windowsill or balcony and again, as they begin to grow, you can snip off your herbs as and when you need them.

Try tarragon, parsley, thyme, coriander (cilantro), chives and basil. Mint has a habit of taking over so it's always best to plant it individually in a separate pot from your other herbs.

HOW TO PLANT YOUR STRAWBERRY POT

Place a layer of stones or gravel at the bottom of the pot and then add potting mix up to the first hole in the pot.

Take your first herb plant out of the plastic container that it came in and ease it into the hole from the outside. Add more potting mix until the herb plant feels secure and you reach the next planting hole. Then add your next herb and repeat with the potting mix.

Keep repeating until all of the holes are filled with herbs and the pot is filled with potting mix up to the top. End by planting a last herb at the top.

Summer

The advent of summer brings longer days in which to socialise, get more projects completed in daylight, both inside the house and out in the garden, and to really start living life outdoors, whether that's in the bonus space of those garden, balcony or terrace 'rooms', or in your nearest park or open space.

Oh the joyous thrill of a bountiful summer's day – from June to September, the season to make you smile! Have you ever seen a field full of sunflowers? If you have then you might have noticed one of nature's most wonderful magic tricks – that the heads of the sunflowers will all be turned in the same direction, at a similar angle and in the same way to face the direct glare of the sun. In fact, if you come back later on in the day – when the sun is lower in the sky – the flowers will have tilted downwards in order to follow the same route taken by the sun. The advent of summer brings longer days in which to socialise, get more projects completed in daylight, both inside the house and out in the garden, and to really start living life outdoors, whether that's in the garden, on the balcony or in terrace 'rooms' or in your nearest park or open space!

It's almost meditative to watch animals and insects go about their business, and in summer there is an abundance to see and watch, whether you're city bound or a countryside dweller.

Summer means that – whether intentionally or not – we are closer to immersing ourselves within nature, which, according to the Mental Health Foundation, is a huge benefit to our mental wellbeing. It doesn't have to be about countryside living, either – believe me when I say that walking to that park bench and sitting for a few moments to watch the city pigeons for a while is good for you. Stop and try it for a moment. It's almost meditative to watch animals and insects go about their business, and in summer there is an abundance to see and watch, whether you're city bound or a countryside dweller. Immersing ourselves in nature has been a proven aide in reducing stress and feelings of frustration and anger for centuries – it makes us feel more relaxed, which in turn improves our confidence and our self-esteem. There's even a term for sitting still or walking slowly through woodland specifically with a view to soaking up the calm and quiet – it's called 'forest bathing' and it is meant to encourage us to connect to the environment and clear the mind. In Japan, where it's known as shinrin-yoku, it's very much encouraged. It's free, it's readily available and you can do it on your own. It's far easier to muster the motivation to do it in the summertime when the sun is calling you and the woodlands are bursting with every green imaginable, and as green is the colour that most symbolises nature, it too induces feelings of harmony and tranquillity – which can only be a positive thing.

For me, summer means that I get to wear pretty dresses and spend most of my time in my garden. It means that my outdoor space becomes an extension of the house, and it means that I get to lay a lot of outdoor dining areas surrounded by nature and sunlight – if I'm lucky with the British weather! When I lived in London, the advent of summer meant the beginning of park life. We would decamp to our local public park, equipped with blankets and hastily packed plastic bags filled with shop-bought sandwiches, a magazine for me and various bagfuls of paraphernalia for the children. In those days, my life was less about making things beautiful, and more about functionality and getting through the weekend, which is totally understandable when you're a tired mother and unable to see through the haze of exhaustion. However, sometimes it's nice to slip in a few simple styling elements and ideas to make these mundane events seem a little more special. A little injection of prettiness can often be just the tonic for a tired soul.

Living life beautifully is a considered approach that we should all take to our living environments, wherever they may be, and summer is a great time to begin. Country gardens, town gardens, balconies, local parks and terraces – as long as we can see a patch of blue sky and feel a sunray touching our skin, then we're good to go.

STYLING

THE ART OF THE PICNIC

I'm known for my creative table settings, but of course not everyone has the outdoor space required to host seated events during the summer months. What everyone does have, however, is the ability to host a picnic in the garden or park. Picnics may seem like a straightforward and pretty basic way to dine, but with a bit of thought and creativity, even the most simple snack eaten outdoors can become something special. I'm sure that we all have nightmare stories of suspiciously warm and curled-up egg sandwiches covered in foil that are then eaten in the rain while seated at splintered benches on family days out. Those foil- and plastic-packed memories may have almost put you off for life, but picnics can be incredibly pretty, glamorous (and sustainably plastic-free) affairs with minimal effort. With a few carefully planned and considered ideas and accessories such as vintage china, real linen napkins sourced from places such as Etsy, and interesting containers for food, you can elevate those old-school family picnics into a magical feast that can compete with the most beautiful dinner parties. Here are my top ten summer picnic styling ideas, as well as some simple menu suggestions to suit every size and occasion.

ALWAYS HAVE A SELECTION OF EITHER BLANKETS, TABLECLOTHS OR FABRIC READY AS YOUR PICNIC BASE

Although there are no rules about sitting on the ground to enjoy your feast à la Manet's *Le Déjeuner sur l'herbe (The Luncheon on the Grass)*, it doesn't hurt to be prepared, and there is nothing more delightful than uplifting the most simple of occasions to create a pretty scene. Regardless of how basic or grand your picnic will be, blankets will naturally supply comfort, but depending on their pattern and colour they can dictate the feel of your picnic in the same way as creating a tablescape for a dining table.

BRING A CITRONELLA CANDLE OR TWO WITH YOU (DON'T FORGET MATCHES OR A LIGHTER!)

Even I have bad memories of picnics that have been spoiled by unwanted flying guests in the form of pesky flies and wasps. Flying insects are repelled by the smell of citronella, and it doesn't hurt that candles also add atmosphere to any outdoor event. For added protection against flying insects as well as mosquitos on your skin, try using oil from the lemon eucalyptus plant. It's easily available online and is another natural choice in the battle to keep our buzzing friends away from the good stuff!

DON'T FORGET THE ATMOSPHERIC LIGHTING

This is a necessary touch even when insects aren't a problem. If you are able to, try to bring along some lanterns or tea lights in holders so that you can picnic into dusk and early evening on those balmy summer evenings.

PRETTY DOESN'T HAVE TO MEAN EXTRAVAGANT

Wrap up your sandwiches in brown baking paper and then tie up the individual packages with twine, string or ribbon, ending with a bow. Little decorative elements like that sound simple, but a pile of sandwiches displayed this way looks wonderful and stylish with minimum effort. You can also carry individual portions of food and salads or puddings in old jam jars with lids. This will keep things super fresh and stop liquids from spilling.

TRY TO USE VINTAGE CHINA

If you're not venturing far from your house, it's lovely to serve up a picnic on real crockery. Whether it's mismatched china or a perfectly complemented set, allow your chicken drumstick and potato salad to sit in elegant style, rather than languish on a soggy paper plate!

FLOWERS ELEVATE EVERY EVENT OR TABLE

It may seem odd to bring along a bunch of flowers on a casual picnic, but you'd be amazed at how pretty they will make your setting look. If your picnic is close to home or in your own garden, then it's an easy decision, just fill a jug and pop the flowers in. Slightly more difficult if you're having to travel to your picnic, but at least flowers are lightweight, can be held in a bag or propped up in your bicycle basket, and now that florists tend to put bunches of flowers in biodegradable plastic pouches filled with water, they won't dry out either.

COORDINATE TO ELEVATE

Keep your colour scheme simple and uncomplicated but do try to coordinate things a little if you want to make your picnic extra special. Try to seek out a 'hero' colour in your tablecloth or blanket and take it from there. You can match your plates and napkins accordingly, and if you do bring flowers, these can complement the colour scheme too.

DON'T FORGET SEASONING

If you're having to travel to your picnic location, you may have packed different dishes in separate containers for ease of transport. It's easy to forget things like seasonings when you do this, so have a checklist of things to bring, and include salt and pepper shakers, but also a small selection of herbs. You can put cut herbs in ziplock bags if you're travelling, but if you're picnicking in the convenience of your garden with access to your kitchen, either bring out your small herb plants in their containers and a pair of small scissors so people can help themselves and snip to taste, or chop up your herbs and place them in small bowls or even egg cups and put them on the picnic table or cloth.

TRANSPORT FOOD IN REUSABLE PACKAGING

If you'd rather not carry lots of picnic paraphernalia, why not pack individual bento-style boxes, with your picnic food already sectioned out for each person? The original and authentic bento box is a single-portion take-out or home-packed meal of Japanese origin. However, you can be inspired by the real thing and get portioned boxes that have sections for different parts of your picnic.

MAKE IT COMFY

Think about what you'll sit on and what you'll eat off! Bring pillows and cushions if you can – as alluring as lying down on grass can be, sometimes the ground can be bumpier and harder than you imagined. Also think about elevating your food and plates off the ground – even when you've brought a blanket. If you happen to have a vintage suitcase or sturdy picnic basket, these can double up as raised tables as well as containers to carry everything in.

COOKING

PERFECT PICNIC RECIPES

So, you're picnic ready. You know your location, you know your theme, you have your blankets, your baskets, your insect repellent ... but what about a few ideas for tasty food? Here are some of my favourite portable food recipes that are small enough to pack away in individual lunchboxes, or can be made in more generous quantities for a larger buffet-style picnic.

APPLE & WALNUT SALAD

The key here is to get that all-important crunch as well as a variety of flavours, which is why I use crisp romaine for its lovely, sweet taste as well as red endive for its slightly bitter edge. Add crisp apples, toasted walnuts and some crumbly blue cheese and you have the perfect combination.

**Serves 6-8 if a side salad /
4 if a main course**

Ingredients

6 tbsp natural yoghurt

½ tsp honey

1 large sweet red apple, chopped

1 sharper green apple (such as Granny Smith), chopped

1 large celery stick, sliced

2 dates, pitted and roughly chopped

1 crisp romaine lettuce (2 cups), chopped (you could also use iceberg)

1 red endive lettuce, chopped (¾ cup)

75g (2½oz/2/3 cup) walnuts, toasted and roughly chopped

Small wedge of gorgonzola cheese (optional)

Sea salt and freshly ground black pepper

Mix the yoghurt and honey together in a large bowl, then add all the chopped and sliced ingredients and toss together using a couple of wooden spoons.

Season to taste with salt and pepper and then crumble over the gorgonzola, if using, and serve – simple as that!

SPICE ISLAND CHICKEN DRUMSTICKS

If I asked my father what was the single most important thing you needed to make his drumsticks taste delicious, he would say 'patience'. You see, it's all in the marinating, which is a level of forward planning and patience that even I admittedly have had to learn how to acquire over the years. When I think of something tasty that I'd like to eat and I have the ingredients, then I want to make it and eat it now. Ideally my parents would marinate their chicken in the fridge overnight and would have to contend with my childlike calls of 'Is it ready yet?' – and that was me as a grown adult. However, if you – like I – haven't always got the time or patience to wait a whole day for your trip to drumstick heaven, then a minimum of four hours in the fridge will do!

The marinade also works really well with cubes of firm tofu for non-meat eaters.

Makes about 16 drumsticks

Ingredients

2kg (4lb 8oz) chicken drumsticks (about 16 drumsticks)

Oil, for brushing

For the marinade:

2 tbsp olive oil

1 tbsp chopped chives

1 tbsp soft dark brown sugar

Sprig of fresh thyme, leaves chopped

1 garlic clove, grated

1 small onion, finely chopped

1 tsp lime juice

1 tsp medium curry powder (I use Bolt's)

1 tsp ground ginger

1 tsp grated nutmeg

1 tsp ground cinnamon

1 tsp ground allspice

¼ tsp freshly ground black pepper

1 tsp salt

1 tbsp tomato ketchup (optional; my parents swear by this but I prefer to leave it out, although it's delicious either way)

Put all the marinade ingredients into a large bowl and mix to combine. Add the chicken drumsticks and turn to coat in the marinade, making sure that it's liberally covering every nook and cranny – use your fingers if you have to, but massage those drumsticks until they're sighing and totally relaxed (my dad's words, not mine!). To make life easier, pour the marinade and drumsticks into a large ziplock bag – you can massage to your heart's content while still keeping your fingers clean.

Allow the chicken to marinate in the fridge for at least four hours, ideally overnight.

When you are ready to cook, preheat the oven to 190°C/170°C fan/375°F/Gas 5 (or fire up your barbecue if you want to cook over hot coals).

Line a large baking tray with foil and brush lightly with oil to prevent sticking. (Alternatively, arrange the drumsticks on a wire rack over a baking tray.) Tip the drumsticks on to the tray and bake in the oven for 50 minutes–1 hour, turning occasionally. Serve with rice and salad.

INFUSING OIL

Make your own dressings by infusing extra virgin olive oil with your windowsill herbs, garlic and black peppercorns. Thyme, rosemary and lemon thyme all work well for a deliciously intense herby flavour.

Wash and dry your herbs completely and lightly bruise or rub them to bring out their flavours. Add to your oil and leave for a few weeks – the longer you wait the more flavoured the oil. The oil will work wonderfully in a salad dressing over a nice green salad for your picnic, drizzled over pasta or lightly toasted French bread, or even as a dip for fresh bread.

SIMPLE BRUSCHETTA

What do you do with any leftover French bread or ciabatta that may be a bit stale?

Grill it for a few minutes, rub it with a garlic clove and drizzle with your infused olive oil. Roughly chop some tomatoes, and pile them on top with a snippet of basil, parsley or – my preference – coriander (cilantro). A simple light picnic bite, quick snack, canapé or starter before a pasta dish.

MINI 'ETON MESS' PAVLOVAS

The story goes that the traditional English dessert of strawberries, whipped cream and meringue that we call Eton Mess was first mentioned in print in 1893, after being served at a cricket match between Harrow School and Eton College. The 'pavlova' meanwhile, although originating in Australia, was named after the Russian ballerina Anna Pavlova, and consists of a large meringue topped with whipped cream and fruit. This amalgamation of treats offers a bite-sized alternative that is as pretty to look at as it is good to eat!

Makes 6

Ingredients

For the meringues:

4 egg whites

225g (8oz/generous 1 cup) caster (superfine) sugar

For the filling and topping:

250ml (1 cup) whipping cream

250g (9oz) mascarpone cheese

2 tbsp icing (confectioner's) sugar

2 tbsp brandy (optional – you can use vanilla extract instead)

250g (9oz) blueberries and raspberries

Preheat the oven to 150°C/130°C fan/300°F/Gas 2 and line a large baking tray with baking paper.

Place the egg whites in a clean, dry bowl and beat with a hand-held electric whisk until soft peaks form. Add the sugar a spoon at a time, whisking in between each addition for about 5 minutes, or until stiff and glossy.

Spoon the mixture on to the baking paper to make six evenly distributed rounds and a smaller extra one. With the bottom of a spoon, create a central dip in each mound. Place in the oven and immediately reduce the temperature to 130°C/110°C fan/250°F/Gas ½ and bake for 40 minutes. Leave to cool for at least 1 hour in the oven with the door partially open (to prevent them cooling down too quickly and cracking).

Meanwhile, whip the cream with an electric mixer until stiff. Gently fold in the mascarpone, icing sugar and brandy, if using.

When the meringues have completely cooled, transfer to a serving plate. They should have a crunchy shell, but a chewy marshmallowy inside. Spoon the cream evenly into the centre of each meringue.

Crumble the smaller meringue and sprinkle on top, along with the blueberries and raspberries.

MAKING

BEAUTIFUL PROJECTS INSPIRED BY NATURE

Mismatched china teacups are one of the most prolific things to be found in second-hand shops and old vintage markets. Drinking tea out of fine bone china has sadly fallen out of fashion – mainly due to the inconvenience of having to wash vintage ones by hand instead of in a dishwasher. Rather than letting these delicate beauties go to waste, I personally love the beauty of the mismatch and will always try to find inventive ways of breathing new life into them. They will of course still look great in their original use at vintage-styled informal and formal tea parties alike. However, what about the ones that have seen better days, or may have a chip or a missing handle? Sometimes their patterns are just too pretty to discard and I am a great believer in waste not want not, make do and mend, so fear not – all is not lost.

TEACUP CITRONELLA CANDLES

Rather than cluttering up your shelves and cupboards with no purpose or reason, you can turn chipped teacups into the prettiest little vessels for tealights and homemade candles. Here is a simple way to make citronella candles to use as attractive wasp and fly repellents when entertaining outdoors.

You can go the whole hog and use any of the numerous candle-making kits that are available out there, and I do sometimes make my own candles in this way. However, an even easier way is to use up the ends and wax from candles you have burned in the past. If you're like me, you probably have candles that have melted almost down to the nub which usually get thrown out. However, a better use is to collect these ends over time to create new candles.

You will need:

* 4 vintage teacups and saucers

* Bonding glue

* Candle wick

* 1 large pan

* 1 smaller pan that can fit comfortably inside a larger one

* Candle ends or wax flakes (you can source these from candle-making suppliers)

* 1 bottle of citronella essential oil

* 8 clothes pegs

Have your selection of china at the ready, complete with saucers. It really doesn't matter if each saucer matches the cup, in fact in my opinion it looks far more charming and better when they don't match! When you've decided which cup will go with which saucer, glue the cup onto the saucer and allow it to stick firmly.

Cut four lengths of wick the height of the teacup plus 1cm (½in) to hang over the top of each cup.

I have a special double-boiler pan for candle-making as you need to ensure that the wax melts slowly and doesn't overheat (wax can be flammable). If you don't have access to a double boiler you can use two saucepans instead – one large and one smaller one that can fit easily inside the first. Pour water a third of a way up the larger pan, making sure that it doesn't rise up over the sides of the smaller pan inside. Place over a low heat.

Drop your wax ends (or flakes) inside the small pan and keep an eye on it while it gently melts. If you've used the ends of candles, pick out the old wicks with tweezers and discard.

Take one of your lengths of wick and clip two clothes pegs horizontally, at an angle, to the cut end. Rest the pegs on the rim of the teacup so that the wick is dangling in the middle of the cup. Make sure that the wick is nearly touching the bottom and is in as straight a line as possible, but has enough length at the top so that it can be lit.

Carefully pour your melted wax into each teacup, until it's about 3cm (1½in) below the rim and leave to set – pegs and all.

Whenever wax sets around a wick, you'll usually get a slight dip. You can melt the leftover wax again and top up with another layer; keep adding another thin layer after each one has set and the wax is flat. When the candle has completely set, remove the pegs.

TEACUP BIRD FEEDER

While we're on the subject of teacups, how about another use for those mismatched beauties? Teacup bird feeders are incredibly easy to make and are a joy to watch in summer. Not only are they a good use of an unused or chipped teacup, but you'll also be helping your natural environment.

You will need:

* A vintage china teacup and saucer

* Strong ceramic glue

* A strong ribbon, chain or inexpensive vintage necklace

* 'S' hook or connecting chain link attachment
  (available from hardware and DIY stores)

* Bird seed

Place the teacup sideways on the saucer so that you can determine where you want it to be. The cup needs to have its back end close to the edge of the saucer, leaving the front with enough surface for bird seed to spill out on.

Glue your teacup to the saucer, following the manufacturer's instructions for the length of time needed. You may need to weigh it down for a while to make sure it glues in the correct place.

When the cup and saucer are stuck fast, loop your chain through the teacup handle and hang over a tree branch, attaching with an 'S' hook or connecting link.

Fill the cup with birdseed. If you feel that the seed is falling out too much, mix the seed with peanut butter or lard – birds enjoy both – and you'll find that it's more likely to stay put while the birds get stuck into their summer feast.

AFTERWORD

I often wish when I had first moved to Hill House that I had received an operating manual on how to remember to be a 'joy seeker', but like any type of growth, to see the best results takes a bit of experimentation and patience. It's certainly not a 'one shoe fits all' practice, and where one person may find their moments of happiness in watching a plant grow from seed, another may just need to be encouraged to take five minutes out of their day to sit quietly and in peace.

The hardest part is often acknowledging when life doesn't feel quite right and believing that you deserve something better. Like an extra dollop of pudding, an extra dollop of self-care can seem like an indulgence – but it isn't. As the mythical Mary Poppins sang in the Sherman Brothers' song, 'A spoonful of sugar helps the medicine go down', and I'd like you to see this book as your spoonful of sugar. It won't make all of your troubles miraculously disappear, but hopefully you might find a few incentives here to help distract your mind from a few of them.

Over the past decade, and with increasing frequency, I have been asked on social media 'how do you stay so happy?' or 'what's your secret to living happily?'. The pursuit of happiness is a very real and prevalent desire. I am always quick to remind people that what they see on social media is a few seconds of a day and a small glimpse of a life – not the fully rounded picture of someone's lived experience. Comparison is certainly the thief of joy and it would be wiser to use social media as a reference folder to spark inspiration rather than as a template to emulate.

However, the truth is that I have taught myself to experience life in a more joyful manner, but the important word to remember here is 'taught'. It's not something that always comes naturally or easily, but like anything else, takes self-discipline, commitment and a realistic sense of expectation of the results.

In a world where the news seems to offer up one tumultuous event after another, and where social injustice and inequality is still sadly rife, it might seem an oversimplification to offer up a recipe here and a styling project there as a form of jolly-hockey-sticks-style antidote. Staying abreast of world issues is of course crucial, but the point is, it was in these bite-sized helpings that I turned my mind towards the beauty all around me and learned to stop focusing solely on the negative.

Use this book in the same way that you would a radio. Tune into it like a happy song when you need a bit of inspiration and an uplift. Time spent away from drama, trauma, worry or sadness is an important part of a journey towards joyful living. In fact, as demonstrated by the Black Joy movement, for some of us, it's important to remember that, just as Audre Lorde defined self-care as a radical act of political warfare, expressing joy can be a political act in itself.

If there's one thing that you can take away from this book it's that you are doing something extraordinary. So remember that whoever you are, wherever you are and whatever you look like, you have every right to be a joyseeker. Enjoy your joyful living.

NOTES

CHAPTER 1: LIVING A JOYFUL LIFE

Abigail Brenner, 'The Benefits of Creative Visualization', *Psychology Today*, June 2016 www.psychologytoday.com/gb/blog/in-flux/201606/the-benefits-creative-visualization

Pinterest www.pinterest.co.uk

Instagram www.instagram.com

Canva www.canva.com

BeFunky www.Befunky.com

Mural www.mural.co

Keri Smith www.kerismith.com

Sophie Robinson www.sophierobinson.co.uk

Royal Horticultural Society www.rhs.org.uk

Huw Richards www.youtube.com/channel/UCeaKRrrpWiQFJJmiuon2WoQ

Cat Bude @cat_in_france

CHAPTER 2: COUNTRY HOUSE STYLE

Country Life magazine www.countrylife.co.uk

Colefax & Fowler www.colefax.com

Ben Pentreath Ltd www.benpentreath.com

Max Rollitt www.maxrollitt.com

Francesca Rowan Plowden www.rowanplowden.com

Carlos Garcia Interiors www.carlosgarciainteriors.com

Kemi @cottagenoir

The Cornrow www.thecornrow.com

Victoria Ford @prepfordwife

CHAPTER 3: THE ART OF VINTAGE HUNTING

House & Garden magazine www.houseandgarden.co.uk

World of Interiors magazine www.worldofinteriors.co.uk

Ian Mankin www.ianmankin.co.uk

Constance Spry www.gardenmuseum.org.uk/exhibitions/constance-spry-and-the-fashion-for-flowers/

Homes & Antiques magazine www.homesandantiques.com

Miller's Antiques Handbook & Price Guide (UK) blog.millersantiquesguide.com

Kovels' Buying and Price Guides (US) www.kovels.com/buying-guides-booklets

WRAP www.wrap.org.uk

Etsy www.etsy.com

eBay www.ebay.co.uk/www.ebay.com

SUMMER

Mental Health Foundation www.mentalhealth.org.uk

FURTHER READING AND RESOURCES

Finding joy in the everyday is an incredibly relevant and timely topic. It's worth making time for, worth working towards, worth setting goals to achieve and definitely worth fighting for.

BOOK RECOMMENDATIONS

Here are some more reading resources to help you along with your own personal journey to living a joyful life:

Happy, Fearne Cotton, Orion Spring, 2017

Joyful, Ingrid Fetell Lee, Rider, 2018

What I Know For Sure, Oprah Winfrey, Macmillan, 2014

Good Vibes, Good Life, Vex King, Hay House, 2018

Creative Visualisation, Shakti Gawain, New World Library, 2020

The Secret, Rhonda Byrne, Simon & Schuster, 2006

Wreck This Journal, Keri Smith, Penguin Books, 2013

GARDENING INSPIRATION

UK

Gardener, blogger and author **Isabelle Palmer** has written several wonderful books on the subject of gardening for small spaces. *The Balcony Gardener, Creative Ideas for Small Spaces* and *Modern Container Gardening* are great guides to get you started on container growing.
You can also follow her on Instagram at @thebalconygardener for daily tips and ideas.

The Royal Horticultural Society is the UK's leading gardening charity, committed to inspiring everyone to grow. www.rhs.org.uk

The National Allotment Society is the leading national organisation upholding the interests and rights of the allotment community across the UK. www.nsalg.org.uk

The National Garden Scheme has details on open gardens, information and inspiration. www.ngs.org.uk

GrowVeg is run by Growing Interactive, a UK-based company providing innovative garden-planning advice and apps. www.growveg.co.uk/guides/planning-a-square-foot-vegetable-garden

INSTAGRAM ACCOUNTS

Jenny Williams @TheLaundryGarden

The Land Gardeners @thelandgardeners

Charlie McCormick @mccormickcharlie

Becky Cole, Natural Living @beckyocole

Paris Alma Flowers @parisalma

Peonies & Posies @peoniesandposies

Clare Nolan @clarenolan

Willow Crossley Creates @willowcrossleycreates

Diana, Growing Greenfields @growing_greenfields

Sean Pritchard Garden Design @sean_anthony_pritchard

US AND CANADA

The **American Community Gardening Association** is a non-profit organisation focused on community gardening. www.communitygarden.org

The Square Foot Gardening Foundation's mission is to encourage gardening, plant-based living, self-sufficiency and low-impact food production. www.squarefootgardening.org

Erin Benzakein, Floret @floretflower

Linda Vater @potagerblog

Garden Answer @gardenanswer

AUSTRALIA

Community Gardens Australia is an organisation linking people interested in city farming and community gardens across Australia. www.communitygarden.org.au

Jenny Rose Innes @jennyroseinnes

Brenton Roberts @brentonrobertsgardendesigns

EUROPE

Urban Green-Blue Grids is an environmental conservation organisation whose mission is to keep our cities and our planet liveable, safe, healthy and attractive. www.urbangreenbluegrids.com/projects/community-gardens-paris/

Urban Allotment Gardens promotes and encourages allotment gardening by providing information, fact sheets and case studies. www.urbanallotments.eu/case-studies/italy.html

Natasja Sadi @cakeatelieramsterdam

VINTAGE INSTAGRAM HOMEWARES TRADERS AND INSPIRATION ACCOUNTS

UK

The Urban Vintage Affair @the_urban_vintage_affair

Sugden and Daughters @sugdenanddaughters

Reclectic Vintage Interiors @reclecticvintageinteriors

Kathryn McFall @cesttoutinteriors

Decorative Antiques UK @decorativeantiquesuk

The Vintage Trader @thevintagetraderuk

The Country Brocante @thecountrybrocante

Susie Blues Rooms @susiebluesrooms

Arthur Swallow Fairs @asfairs

Brownrigg Interiors and Decorative Antiques @brownrigguk

Liz Morris @lizmorrisdecorativeinteriors

US

White Flower Farmhouse @whiteflowerfarmhouse

Barnhouse Market @barnhousechicksmarket

Chairish @chairishco

Dreamy Whites Lifestyle @dreamywhitelifestyle

The Makerista @themakerista

Liz Marie/Cozy Cottage Style @lizmariegalvan

AUSTRALIA

The Black Hen @theblackhen

Empire Revival @empire.revival

The Vintage & Country Brocante
@thevintageandcountrybrocante

FRANCE

Madame de la Maison
@madamedelamaison

Cat Bude @cat_in_france

Vivi et Margo @vivietmargot

My French Country Home @sharonsantoni

COOKING RESOURCES

Grams to cups converter
www.gramstocups.net

What's Cooking America conversion
www.whatscookingamerica.net/equiv.htm

JOYFUL INSTAGRAMMERS WHO EMBRACE THEIR OWN PERSONAL VINTAGE STYLE

Dandy Wellington @dandywellington

Hen House Homemade
@henhousehomemade

Mars Dilbert @life_on_mars96

Lydia 1940s Vintage Clothing
@lydia1940s Dr Colleen Darnell
@vintage_egyptologist

Vintage Black Glamour
@vintageblackglamour

Zack Pinsent @pinsent_tailoring

Angelique Noire @the_angelique_noire

Jessica Kellgren-Fozard
@jessicaoutofthecloset

INSPIRING INSTAGRAMMERS FOR COUNTRY AND VINTAGE INTERIORS

Louisa at Starre Corner
@elegantlyknackeredstyle

Lisa Dawson @_lisa_dawson_

Lisa Piddington @lisa_loves_vintage

Kemi @cottagenoir

Dee Campling @deecampling

Victoria Ford @prepfordwife

No Feature Walls @nofeaturewalls

Carlos Garcia Interiors
@carlosgarciainteriors@tamsynmorgans

Amanda Skipper @thevintagerose_

Bee Osborn @osborninteriors

INSPIRING INSTAGRAM ACCOUNTS FOR UPCYCLING AND RECYCLING

Africa Daley-Clarke @thevitamindproject

Grillo Designs @grillodesigns

Melanie Lissack Interiors
@melanielissackinteriors

SPECIAL MENTIONS

Kate Watson Smythe
@mad_about_the_house
www.madaboutthehouse.com

Candice Braithwaite @candicebrathwaite
www.alldressedupwithnowheretogo.com

Medina Grillo @grillodesigns
www.grillo-designs.com

THANK YOU

Marianne Tatepo at Penguin Random House – for believing in me, guiding me and holding my hand through each part of the process.

Simon Brown – for seeing the beauty that I see and bringing it alive in the most spectacular way.

Dave Brown at Apeinc.co.uk – for art directing a book that looks good enough to eat!

Megan Staunton at Gleam Titles – for helping me believe that I could do it.

Amelia Bell and Lauren Clark at Gleam Futures – for being the best cheerleaders.

Lucy Loveridge at Gleam Futures – for taking a chance and starting me on this incredible journey.

Tamsyn Morgans – for being a constant source of friendship, support and style.

Nina Fuga – for bringing the magic of Hill House to life through illustration.

Clare Sayer – for being a fountain of knowledge, plus reminding me to dot my 'i's and cross my 't's with kind diplomacy!

Huxley Ogilvy – for always being so cheerful on shoots, even when holding my skirt!

Coco – for being the star they really want to see!

A

allotments 44
amaryllis 172
antiques 8, 51, 57, 92
  'antique' labelling 97
  durability 50, 93
  guides 84, 96
  mixing with modern 49, 90–1
  updating 91
  value 80, 93
antiques emporiums 79, 102
antiques markets 13, 84, 101
antiques shops, local 78, 102
apple & walnut salad 228
art deco 107
art nouveau 107
arts and crafts 107
auctions and auction houses 13, 63, 79, 101, 103
autumn 120, 124–57
  cooking 140–9
  making 150–7
  styling 130–9
autumn wreaths 213

B

bento boxes 221
bird feeder, teacup 241
Black interior styles 59–60
Black Joy movement 243
blankets 135, 157, 221
body butter, homemade whipped 185–6
Bonfire Night 141
Brenner, Abigail 22
bruschetta, simple 233
Bude, Cat 45
bulbs
  indoor potted 42, 170–1
  spring pots and planters 197
Byrne, Rhonda 23

C

cabbageware 136, 202
candelabras 152–5, 203
candles
  citronella 222, 237–9
  for dining table 203
  in jam jars 155, 203
  scented 157

candlesticks 91, 152–5, 203
car boot sales 13, 63, 101, 102–3
carbon footprint 93
Caribbean 8, 41, 50, 60, 142, 172
cheese & charcuterie display board, easy 208–11
chestnut leek & mushroom tartlets 144–5
china see vintage china
chintz 50, 51, 54, 80
Christmas 135, 161, 172, 212, 213
citronella candles 222
  teacup 237–9
classic snowball 168
clothes 31–7
  colours 38
  vintage 37, 81
cocoa butter 185–6
Colefax & Fowler 54
colours
  autumn 126, 132, 136, 138
  butter yellow 54
  clothing 38
  coordinating for picnics 223
  interiors 38
  spring 199, 202
comfort 47, 51, 54, 57, 58, 62, 126, 161
  country house style rule 67
  picnics 135, 221
conkers 137, 188
conkie 142–3
Constance Spry planters 84–5
container gardening 42
corn dolls 131
cosiness 62, 126, 151, 161, 162
cosy reading nooks 155–6
  checklist 157
cottagecore 49, 62–4, 126
country brocante 102–3
country house style 46–73
  old guard 54–5
  and race 58–60
  relevance of cottagecore 62–4
  rules for the modern home 67–72
  today 56–7
Country Life 8, 50

creating, joy of 41
creative visualisation 22–7

D

daffodils 197, 198
dresses 34, 36
durability 93

E

eBay 13, 91, 101, 103, 155
  bidding tips 104
entrances, styling 197
environmentalism 64
Etsy 101, 155, 221

F

fabric
  napkin making 200
  as a picnic base 221
  and re-upholstery 80, 99, 108
  reflecting the seasons 138
fairy lights 155
fake grass table mats 199
faking it 138
festoon lights 155
flocked rabbits 201, 203
flowers
  indoor potted bulbs 42, 170–2
  re-using 134
  spring 195, 196–8, 212–14
  as a spring centerpiece 203
  for summer picnics 223
forest bathing (shinrin-yoku) 218–19
Fowler, John 50–1, 54
framed collections 91
frames, checking 98
Freecycle 101
fresh air breaks 163
Fulham Pottery 84–5
functionality 67–8
furniture see vintage furniture

G

Garcia, Carlos 57
garden candlelight 151–5
garden chandelier 151–2
gardening
  joy of growing 41–4
  raised-bed gardens 24, 42–3

Gawain, Shakti 23
gourds 134–5
Grandmother's Chest 81, 86–7
Grenada 41, 142, 177

H
Halloween 134–5
happiness 13, 20–1, 22, 23, 33, 64, 163, 194, 242–3
    and colour 38
    outside our comfort zone 45
    and personal style 37
Harvest Festival 131
herbs
    homegrown in vintage pots 214–15
    infusing oil 232
    for picnics 221
high street shops 102
Hill House 8, 12, 13–15
    description 48
    the seasons at 118–23, 151, 162
Hill House Living 16–111
Hill House Vintage 48, 162
    becoming 78–85
    and cottagecore 62–3
hot drinks 157
'Hunford' 8, 9
hurricane jars 203
hyacinths 42, 171–2
hygge 126

I
infusing oil 232
insect repellants 222, 237–9
Instagram 7, 33, 37, 80, 101, 151
interior styles timeline 106–7

J
journaling 27
joy 7, 13–14, 15
    of creating and growing 41–4
    joy seeking 242–3
    living a joyful life 18–45

K
Kemi@cottagenoir 60
Kensington Market 81
Kovel's 96

L
Lancaster, Nancy 50–1, 54–5, 67, 68, 72
lanterns 155, 203, 222
lighting
    candlelight in the garden 151–5
    outdoor picnics 222
London 6, 7, 8, 20–1, 31, 78, 116, 120, 131, 141, 144, 219
Lorde, Audre 243

M
'make do and mend' 8, 64, 237
Mankin, Ian 80
measurements 96
mid-century modern 81, 107
Miller's Antiques 84, 96
mixing it up 13, 49, 72, 81, 90–1
modernism 107
mood boards 22, 23–7, 34
    creating 26–7
moth infestations 96
muscari ('Grape Hyacinth') 197, 198

N
name cards 201
napkins and napkin rings, spring 200
nature-inspired decorations 132
Norfolk 6, 7, 12, 20, 31, 48, 78, 117, 131

O
oat milk rice pudding 177
oil, infusing 232
online mood board makers 27
online vintage hunting 101
outdoor eating 194, 219
    autumn picnics 135
    summer picnics 220–3

P
pantry suppers 175–81
paperwhite narcissus 42, 170–1
Paula's easy leftovers cheese soufflé 178

pavlovas, mini Eton Mess 234
Pentreath, Ben 57
personal style 31–8
    checklist 34–7
    colours 38
Physalis alkekengi 137
picnics
    autumn 135
    summer 220–4
pine cones 137, 188, 189, 213
Pinterest 27
pot pourri, winter 188–9
potted bulbs 42, 170–2, 197
produce, autumnal 131

Q
quiet spaces/nooks 28–9
    checklist 29

R
race
    and country house style 58–60
    and vintage clothing 37
raised-bed gardens 24, 42–3
re-upholstering 80, 99, 108–9
Richards, Huw 42–4
Robinson, Sophie 38
Rollitt, Max 57
Rowan Plowden, Francesca 57

S
Sackville-West, Vita 36
sandwich wrappings 222
saying 'yes' 45
scale 68
scrapbooking 26
seasoning, for picnics 221
seasons 13–15, 112–241
    at Hill House 118–23
self-care 20, 28, 33, 64, 156, 199, 242, 243
shea butter 185–6
Shiva and Shakti 22
silver hallmarks 98
slavery 59
'slow decorator' 15, 24, 57, 78
socks 157
Spice Island chicken drumsticks 230–1
spring 121, 192–215
    cooking 204–11

making 212–15
styling 196–203
spring flowers 195
    floral ideas 196–7
    getting to know 198
    tribute to 212–15
spring wreaths 213
Spry, Constance 84
square-foot gardening 42–4
strawberry pots, planting 215
Sugden, Louisa 49–50
summer 121, 216–41
    cooking 226–35
    making 236–41
    styling 220–5
summer wreaths 214
sustainability 92–3
sweet tomato & onion relish 149

T

table setting
    autumn 134, 136
    spring 199–203
table-setting baskets 201
tablecloths 136, 138, 221
tableware, choosing for spring
    201
tea lights 155, 203, 222
teacups, mismatched 237
    teacup bird feeder 241
    teacup citronella candles
    237–9
textiles
    autumnal 136, 138
    checking for moths 96
tryptophan 157
tulips 197, 198

U

understatement 68
uniqueness 92
upcycling
    garden chandelier 151–2
    re-upholstering a chair 198–9
    upcycled vintage project
    80–1

V

value 93
vegetable growing 41, 42–4,
    126
Victoria@prepfordwife 60

Victoria sponge cake 206–7
Victorian button-backed chair
    project 80, 82–3
Victorian puff pastry pies
180–1
vintage 8, 13, 48, 51, 57, 58, 63
    mixing with modern 49, 81
    90–1
    origins of the word 75
    see also Hill House vintage;
vintage hunting
vintage baskets 131
vintage candelabras and
candlesticks 152–5
vintage china
    blue and white 79
    cracks and chips 97
    dining sets 201
    mismatched teacup projects
    237–41
    for picnics 223
    serving platters 205, 210
vintage clothing 37, 58, 81
vintage collections, displaying
    130
    framing 91
    organising by 'families' 132
vintage containers (pots, bowls
    and jugs) 170, 171, 201, 208,
    211, 214–15
vintage emporiums 13, 102
vintage furniture
    1930s–1960s 97
    curves and angles 90
    inherited 81
    ripped 99
    scale 68
    solid-wood 48
    as storytelling 72
    sustainability 92–3
    upcycling 80–1, 108–9
    woodworm 98
vintage glassware 166
vintage hunting 74–109
    3 'F's 100
    becoming Hill House vintage
    78–89
    beginning 100–3
    eBay bidding guide 104
    Hill House guide 92–104
    Paula's top ten tips for
buying 96–9

reasons to go vintage 92–3
vintage markets 63, 102–3
vintage mirrors 98
vintage paintings 98
vintage shops 76, 79, 80, 102,
    201
vintage textiles 138
    checking for moths 96

W

wellbeing 13, 20–1, 28, 44, 121,
    162
    and daylight 163
    and flowers and plants 195
    and immersion in nature
    218–19
    and personal style 31–3, 37
    and quiet spaces 28
    winter wellbeing projects
    185–9
Wellington, Dandy 37
window boxes 197
Windrush generation 58
Winfrey, Oprah 23
winter 116, 120, 160–91
    cooking 174–83
    making 184–9
    styling 164–73
winter/Christmas wreaths 213
winter warmer bar cart 166–7
woodworm 98
'word of the year' 45
work-life balance 20–1, 64
wreaths 212–14

Y

YouTube 27, 63, 151

1

Ebury Press, an imprint of Ebury Publishing,
20 Vauxhall Bridge Road, London SW1V 2SA

Ebury Press is part of the Penguin Random House group
of companies whose addresses can be found at
global.penguinrandomhouse.com

First published by Ebury Press in 2021

www.penguin.co.uk

A CIP catalogue record for this book is available from the British Library

ISBN 9781529109658

Text Design: Dave Brown, APE Inc.
Styling: Paula Sutton
Photography: Simon Brown
Photographer's Assistant: Huxley Ogilvy
Illustrations: Nina Fuga

Colour origination by Altaimage London
Printed and bound in China by C&C Offset Printing Co., Ltd

The authorised representative in the EEA is Penguin Random House
Ireland, Morrison Chambers, 32 Nassau Street, Dublin D02 YH68.

Penguin Random House is committed to a sustainable future for our
business, our readers and our planet. This book is made from Forest
Stewardship Council® Certified paper.

Photo by Tamsyn Morgans

Paula Sutton is a stylist, writer and creator of popular blog and Instagram, Hill House Vintage. A born and bred south Londoner, having trained as a Town & Country Planner, she worked at ELLE as Bookings Editor and Elite models as Head of Press. *Hill House Living* is her first book.

Website: hillhousevintage.com

Instagram: @hillhousevintage

Twitter: @hillhousevintag

Facebook: @hillhousevintage